Published by
Rupa Publications India Pvt. Ltd 2025
7/16, Ansari Road, Daryaganj
New Delhi 110002

Sales centres:
Bengaluru Chennai
Hyderabad Jaipur Kathmandu
Kolkata Mumbai Prayagraj

Copyright © Rupa Publications India Pvt. Ltd 2025

The views and opinions expressed in this book are the
authors' own and the facts are as reported by him which
have been verified to the extent possible, and the publishers
are not in any way liable for the same.

All rights reserved.
No part of this publication may be reproduced, transmitted,
or stored in a retrieval system, in any form or by any means,
electronic, mechanical, photocopying, recording or otherwise,
without the prior permission of the publisher.

Photo Source: Wikimedia Commons

ISBN: 978-93-6156-595-3

First impression 2025

10 9 8 7 6 5 4 3 2 1

The moral right of the author has been asserted.

Printed in India

This book is sold subject to the condition that it shall not,
by way of trade or otherwise, be lent, resold, hired out, or otherwise
circulated, without the publisher's prior consent, in any form of
binding or cover other than that in which it is published.

CONTENTS

Introduction   5

1. The History and Evolution of Swimming   7

SECTION ONE
GETTING STARTED

2. Understanding Swimming as a Sport   20
3. Essential Gear and Equipment   31
4. The Basics of Water Safety   40

SECTION TWO
LEARNING THE FUNDAMENTALS

5. Getting Comfortable in the Water   50
6. Introduction to the Four Competitive Strokes   55

SECTION THREE
MASTERING EACH STROKE

7. Freestyle (Front Crawl)   62

8.	Backstroke	69
9.	Breaststroke	75
10.	Butterfly	81

SECTION FOUR
ADVANCED TECHNIQUES AND TRAINING

11.	Starts, Turns, and Finishes	88
12.	Developing Endurance and Speed	96
13.	Strength Training for Swimmers	101
14.	Nutrition, Rest, and Injury Prevention for Swimmers	108
15.	Nurturing a Future Olympic Swimmer	111
16.	Filipino Olympians in Swimming: Spirit in Olympic Waters	114

List of Olympic Medalists in Swimming (2000-2024) 121

INTRODUCTION

SWIMMING, AN EXHILARATING AND VERSATILE SPORT, offers both competitive excitement and recreational enjoyment. This introduction delves into the essence of swimming as a sport, emphasizing its appeal, the skills required, and its position in the contemporary athletic landscape.

Swimming stands out as one of the most accessible and inclusive sports, welcoming participants of all ages and skill levels. Whether practiced in a local pool or performed on the grand stage of international competitions, swimming provides a unique combination of physical challenge and grace. The sport is celebrated for its ability to enhance cardiovascular fitness, build muscular strength, and improve overall flexibility, all while being gentle on the joints.

Modern swimming encompasses a variety of styles and distances, each with its own set of techniques and strategies. The primary strokes—freestyle, backstroke, breaststroke, and butterfly—each offer distinct challenges and opportunities for personal expression. Freestyle, known for its speed and efficiency, is often the focus of sprint events and long-distance races. Backstroke, performed on the back, combines elements of speed and technique with a unique breathing rhythm. Breaststroke, characterized by its distinctive frog-like kick and arm movement, requires precise timing and coordination. Butterfly, the most demanding stroke, tests swimmers' strength and stamina through its powerful, undulating motion.

Competitive swimming has evolved significantly, with swimmers now employing advanced techniques and training methods to gain a competitive edge. The sport has embraced cutting-edge technology, including high-tech swimsuits designed to reduce drag and enhance performance. Swimwear innovations, along with improvements in pool design and timing systems, have contributed to the setting of new world records and the pushing of human limits.

In addition to its competitive aspect, swimming is widely recognized for its therapeutic benefits. The low-impact nature of the sport makes it an ideal choice for rehabilitation and injury prevention. Swimmers benefit from a full-body workout that strengthens muscles, improves cardiovascular health, and promotes overall well-being. The calming effects of water also contribute to mental relaxation and stress relief, making swimming a popular choice for both fitness enthusiasts and those seeking a serene, meditative experience.

As the world of swimming evolves, the sport remains a dynamic and ever-changing discipline. Its blend of physical challenge, technical skill, and universal appeal ensures that swimming will continue to captivate and inspire both participants and spectators for years to come.

1

THE HISTORY AND EVOLUTION OF SWIMMING

SWIMMING, AS A SPORT AND ACTIVITY, BOASTS A **rich** and multifaceted history that spans centuries. This chapter explores the origins of swimming, its development into a competitive sport, notable swimmers and milestones, and its current role in global sports. Through this exploration, we gain insight into how swimming has evolved and continues to captivate athletes and spectators alike.

ORIGINS OF SWIMMING AS A SPORT

The origins of swimming can be traced back to ancient civilizations where it was practiced both as a survival skill and a form of recreation. Evidence of early swimming practices is found in various ancient cultures, highlighting its significance across different regions and epochs.

Ancient Civilizations

- **Ancient Egypt:** Artifacts and murals from ancient Egypt, dating back to around 2000 BCE, depict individuals swimming in the Nile River. The Egyptians valued swimming not only as a recreational activity but also as a vital skill for navigating the river and engaging in various water-related tasks. These early representations suggest that swimming was an integral part of their daily life.

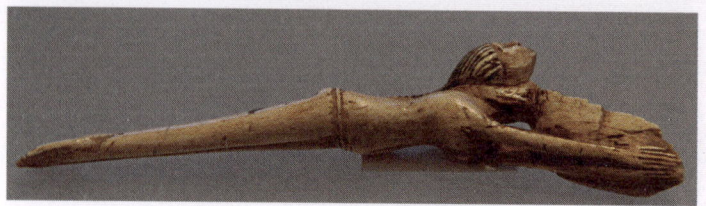

Ancient Egypt Gallery, Louvre Museum, Paris, France

- **Ancient Greece and Rome:** The Greeks and Romans further advanced the practice of swimming. The Greeks incorporated swimming into their physical education system, emphasizing it as a crucial aspect of their training for athletic competitions. Swimming was a common feature in the gymnasiums and public baths of ancient Greece. Similarly, the Romans built elaborate bathhouses with swimming pools, known as "piscinae," which were central to social and cultural life. The Romans' engineering prowess contributed to the development of sophisticated swimming facilities.

THE HISTORY AND EVOLUTION OF SWIMMING

Roman Piscine

Medieval and Renaissance Periods

- **Medieval Europe:** During the medieval period, swimming saw a decline in popularity in Europe. This decline was partly due to the societal shift towards more sedentary lifestyles and the negative associations of swimming with disease and uncleanliness. However, swimming continued to be practiced in other parts of the world, such as in the Middle East and Asia, where it remained a valued activity.
- **Renaissance Revival:** The Renaissance period marked a resurgence in interest in swimming, driven by a renewed focus on physical education and the study of classical texts. Figures such as German physician Nikolaus Wynmann, who wrote "Der Schwimmer oder ein Zwiegespräch über die Schwimmkunst" (The Swimmer or a Dialogue on the Art of Swimming) in 1538, contributed to the revival of swimming as both a sport and a health practice. Wynmann's work is considered one of the earliest known treatises on swimming.

DEVELOPMENT OF COMPETITIVE SWIMMING

The transformation of swimming from a recreational activity to a competitive sport occurred gradually over the 19th and early 20th centuries. This period saw the formalization of rules, the establishment of organizations, and the organization of competitions, all of which contributed to the development of competitive swimming as we know it today.

Early Competitions

- **The 19th Century:** Competitive swimming began to take shape in the 19th century, with the formation of swimming clubs and the organization of local races. In Australia, the first recorded swimming competition took place in 1846, and by the 1850s, swimming competitions were being held in the United Kingdom and the United States. These early competitions were often held in natural bodies of water, such as rivers and lakes, before the advent of modern swimming pools.

Surf-Swimming, Sandwich Islands (page out of Captain Cook's Voyages round the World, 1897)

Mermaids at Brighton by William Heath, 1829

- **Standardization of Strokes:** The late 19th and early 20th centuries saw the standardization of swimming strokes, which played a crucial role in formalizing competitive swimming. The freestyle (or front crawl) stroke, developed by indigenous Australians and Polynesians, became popular due to its speed and efficiency. The backstroke, breaststroke, and butterfly strokes were also formalized during this period, each contributing to the diversity of competitive events.

Formation of Governing Bodies

- **International Swimming Federation (FINA):** The International Swimming Federation, or FINA, was founded in 1908, serving as the global governing body for competitive swimming. FINA's role in standardizing rules, organizing international competitions, and promoting the sport on a global scale

Former FINA logo

was pivotal in shaping modern competitive swimming. The organization's influence extends to setting world records, regulating swimwear technology, and ensuring fair play in competitions.

Modern Era and Innovations

- **Technological Advancements:** The late 20th and early 21st centuries witnessed significant technological advancements that transformed competitive swimming. Innovations such as high-tech swimsuits, advanced pool designs, and electronic timing systems have enhanced performance and accuracy in competitions. For example, the introduction of polyurethane swimsuits in the early 2000s led to numerous world records, although their use was later restricted by FINA to ensure fairness.

Woman's Swimming Costume in Early 20th Century

Swimming Shorts for Men in Mid-20th Century

People relaxing by the swimming pool, 20th Century

- **Inclusion in the Olympics:** Swimming has been a part of the Olympic Games since the inaugural modern Olympics in 1896. The sport's inclusion in the Olympics provided a prestigious platform for swimmers to showcase their skills on a global stage. The Olympics have since become the premier event for competitive swimming, featuring a wide range of events and attracting top swimmers from around the world.

Modern Olympics in 1896

NOTABLE SWIMMERS AND MILESTONES

Throughout its history, swimming has been graced by numerous exceptional athletes whose achievements have shaped the sport and inspired future generations. These swimmers have set world records, won Olympic medals, and contributed to the sport's rich legacy.

Michael Phelps

- **Achievements:** Michael Phelps, often regarded as one of the greatest swimmers of all time, has had an unparalleled impact on the sport. With 23 Olympic gold medals and numerous world records, Phelps' career is marked by extraordinary

Michael Phelps

achievements in events such as the 100m butterfly, 200m freestyle, and 400m individual medley. His dominance in swimming, combined with his work ethic and dedication, has left an indelible mark on the sport.

- **Legacy:** Phelps' influence extends beyond his competitive success. He has been an advocate for mental health awareness and has contributed to the development of swimming programs and initiatives aimed at promoting the sport. His legacy continues to inspire swimmers at all levels to pursue excellence and push the boundaries of their performance.

Katie Ledecky

- **Achievements:** Katie Ledecky is another remarkable swimmer who has achieved great success in freestyle events. Ledecky's dominance in distance swimming is highlighted by her multiple world records and Olympic gold medals. Her performances in events such as the 800m and 1500m freestyle have set new standards in the sport and showcased her exceptional talent and endurance.

Katie Ledecky

- **Impact:** Ledecky's contributions to swimming extend beyond her competitive success. She has become a role model for young swimmers and has used her platform to promote the sport and support various charitable causes. Her dedication and achievements have solidified her place as one of the sport's leading figures.

Other Notable Swimmers

- **Mark Spitz:** Mark Spitz, with his nine Olympic gold medals, was a dominant force in swimming during the late 1960s and early 1970s. Spitz's achievements included setting world records in multiple events, and his performance at the 1968 and 1972 Olympics remains legendary.
- **Ian Thorpe:** Ian Thorpe, known as "Thorpedo," made significant contributions to swimming with his success in freestyle events. Thorpe's career is marked by multiple Olympic gold medals and world records, and he remains one of the sport's most celebrated athletes.

Mark Spitz 1967

Ian Thorpe

THE ROLE OF SWIMMING IN GLOBAL SPORTS

Swimming plays a prominent role in the global sports landscape, with its presence in major international competitions, its widespread popularity, and its influence on health and fitness.

International Competitions

- **Olympics:** Swimming is a central feature of the Olympic Games, showcasing top swimmers from around the world. The Olympics provide a prestigious platform for athletes to compete at the highest level and achieve international recognition. Events such as the 100m freestyle, 200m butterfly, and 400m medley highlight the sport's diversity and complexity.

1904 Olympics – First heat of the fifty yard swimming Olympic Championship

Men's Swimming Race at the 1912 Summer Olympics

THE HISTORY AND EVOLUTION OF SWIMMING

Women's Freestyle Swimming Race at the 1912 Summer Olympics

- **World Championships:** The FINA World Swimming Championships, held biennially, offer another major platform for swimmers to compete and set records. These championships attract top athletes and provide opportunities for emerging swimmers to gain international experience.

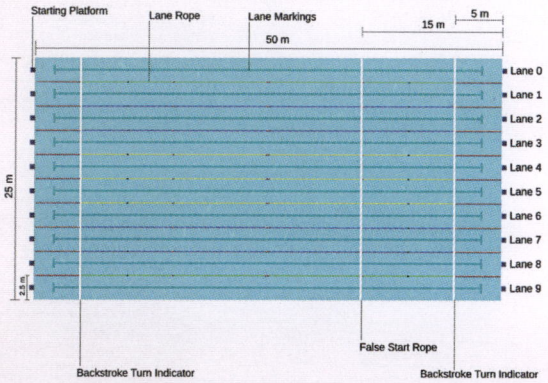

Simplified Diagram of the FINA long course swimming pool standard

OLYMPIC SERIES: SWIMMING

Stamps of Germany (Berlin) 1978

The history and evolution of swimming reflect its journey from ancient recreational activity to a globally recognized sport. The development of competitive swimming, the achievements of notable swimmers, and the sport's role in global sports underscore its significance and enduring appeal. As swimming continues to evolve, its rich history and ongoing advancements will shape its future and inspire new generations of athletes.

SECTION ONE

GETTING STARTED

2

UNDERSTANDING SWIMMING AS A SPORT

SWIMMING IS BOTH AN ART AND A SCIENCE, combining elements of athleticism, technique, and endurance. It involves moving through water using a combination of body movements and strokes. Swimming is distinguished by its ability to provide a full-body workout that engages multiple muscle groups, improves cardiovascular health, and enhances flexibility. The sport is practiced in various settings, including pools, open water bodies, and specialized therapeutic environments.

At its core, swimming involves propelling oneself through water using a series of strokes, each with its unique technique and purpose. The basic strokes—freestyle, backstroke, breaststroke, and butterfly—are fundamental to competitive swimming and are also commonly used in recreational and therapeutic contexts. Each stroke offers different benefits and challenges, contributing to the sport's diversity and appeal.

Swimming can be performed in different environments, including:

- **Pools:** The most common setting for swimming, where controlled conditions allow for structured training and competition.

Swimming Pool

- **Open Water:** Includes lakes, rivers, and oceans, providing a more challenging environment with varying conditions.

Swimming Hole of the Wisconsin River

- **Therapeutic Settings:** Specialized pools and facilities designed for rehabilitation and therapeutic purposes.

Hydrotherapy Session

TYPES OF SWIMMING: COMPETITIVE, RECREATIONAL, AND THERAPEUTIC

Competitive Swimming

Competitive swimming is the most structured form of the sport, involving organized races and events where swimmers compete against each other to achieve the fastest times. Key features of competitive swimming include:

- **Structured Events:** Swimmers compete in various distances and strokes, including sprints (e.g., 50m freestyle), middle-distance (e.g., 200m individual medley), and long-distance races (e.g., 1500m freestyle).
- **Governing Bodies:** Organizations like the International Swimming Federation (FINA) set the rules and regulations for competitive swimming and organize major international events such as the Olympics and World Championships.

UNDERSTANDING SWIMMING AS A SPORT

- **Training and Technique:** Competitive swimmers undergo rigorous training to improve their technique, speed, and endurance. Training programs often include interval workouts, technique drills, and strength conditioning.

Competitive Swimming

Recreational Swimming

Recreational swimming focuses on enjoyment, fitness, and relaxation rather than competition. It is accessible to people of all ages and skill levels and offers numerous benefits, including:

- **Fitness and Wellness:** Recreational swimming provides a low-impact cardiovascular workout, helping to improve overall fitness and well-being. It is often used as a form of exercise for maintaining health and managing weight.

- **Social and Recreational Activities:** Many people swim for leisure, relaxation, or social interaction. Recreational swimming can be done in community pools, beach settings, or private swim clubs.
- **Skill Development:** Recreational swimmers often engage in lessons or group sessions to improve their swimming skills and techniques for enjoyment and safety.

Recreational Swimming

Therapeutic Swimming

Therapeutic swimming, also known as aquatic therapy, utilizes water-based exercises and activities to promote physical and mental health. It is used for:

- **Rehabilitation:** Aquatic therapy is commonly used in rehabilitation settings to aid recovery from injuries, surgeries, or chronic conditions. The buoyancy of water reduces stress on joints and supports gentle movement.
- *Pain Management*: Water-based exercises can alleviate pain and improve mobility for individuals with conditions such as arthritis or fibromyalgia.

- **Improving Function:** Therapeutic swimming helps individuals enhance their physical function, strength, and flexibility in a supportive environment.

Aquatic Therapy

BASIC RULES AND REGULATIONS OF SWIMMING

Understanding the basic rules and regulations of swimming is essential for participants and spectators alike. These rules ensure fair competition, safety, and consistency across different levels of the sport.

General Rules

- **Starting and Finishing:** In competitive swimming, races typically start with a dive from the poolside or starting blocks. Swimmers must touch the wall at the end of each length or race to complete the event. Touching the wall with any part of the body is acceptable, depending on the stroke being performed.

- **Stroke Specific Rules:** Each swimming stroke has specific rules that dictate the technique and movements allowed. For example, in freestyle, swimmers can use any arm and leg movements, while in breaststroke, both arms must move simultaneously in a specific manner, and the legs must perform a frog kick.
- **Disqualifications:** Swimmers can be disqualified for various infractions, including false starts, improper stroke techniques, or failure to touch the wall correctly. Disqualifications result in the swimmer being removed from the race and their time not being recorded.

Competition Rules

- **Lane Assignments:** In pool competitions, swimmers are assigned specific lanes to ensure fair competition. Each lane is marked to prevent swimmers from encroaching on each other's space.
- **Timing and Judging:** Electronic timing systems are used to record swimmers' times accurately. Judges and referees oversee the races to ensure compliance with the rules and address any violations.
- **Relay Races:** Relay races involve teams of swimmers competing together. Each swimmer must complete their leg of the race before the next swimmer can start, and precise baton exchanges are crucial for a successful relay.

OVERVIEW OF DIFFERENT SWIMMING EVENTS

Swimming events vary in distance, stroke, and format, each offering unique challenges and excitement. Understanding these events provides insight into the diversity of competitive swimming and the skills required to excel.

Individual Events

- **Freestyle (or Front Crawl):** The freestyle is the fastest and most popular stroke, characterized by an alternating arm movement and a flutter kick. Races are held over various distances, including sprints (50m, 100m) and long-distance events (200m, 400m, 800m, 1500m).

Freestyle

- **Backstroke:** Swimmers perform the backstroke while lying on their back, using a flutter kick and alternating arm movements. Events are typically held in 100m, 200m, and 400m distances.
- **Breaststroke:** The breaststroke involves a frog-like arm movement and a distinctive frog kick. It requires precise timing and coordination and is raced over distances of 100m and 200m.

Backstroke Breaststroke

- **Butterfly:** Known for its demanding technique, the butterfly stroke involves simultaneous arm movements and a dolphin kick. Races are held over 100m and 200m distances.

Butterfly Stroke

INDIVIDUAL MEDLEY (IM)

The Individual Medley involves all four strokes (butterfly, backstroke, breaststroke, and freestyle) in a single race. Swimmers must transition smoothly between strokes, making the IM a test of versatility and endurance. Distances include 200m and 400m.

Relay Events

- **Freestyle Relay:** Teams of four swimmers each swim a specified distance in freestyle. The relay format includes 4x50m, 4x100m, and 4x200m events.
- **Medley Relay:** Each swimmer in a team performs a different stroke (backstroke, breaststroke, butterfly, freestyle) in a specified order. The relay includes 4x100m and 4x200m events.

OPEN WATER SWIMMING

Open water swimming takes place in natural bodies of water such as lakes, rivers, and oceans. Events vary in distance, with races commonly held over 5km, 10km, and 25km. Open water swimming presents additional challenges, including navigation, varying water conditions, and the need for endurance.

MARATHON SWIMMING

Marathon swimming is an endurance discipline involving long-distance races in open water, often exceeding 25km. These events test swimmers' stamina and adaptability to challenging conditions, such as cold water and currents.

Understanding swimming as a sport involves recognizing its diverse forms, from competitive racing to recreational and therapeutic swimming. Knowledge of basic rules, regulations, and different swimming events enhances one's appreciation of the sport and its multifaceted nature. As swimming continues to evolve, its various aspects offer a rich and rewarding experience for athletes and enthusiasts alike.

3

ESSENTIAL GEAR AND EQUIPMENT

IN SWIMMING, HAVING THE RIGHT GEAR AND EQUIPMENT can significantly impact performance, comfort, and overall enjoyment. This chapter explores the essential gear needed for swimming, including swimsuits, goggles, swim caps, and other accessories. It also covers pool equipment and offers tips on caring for your gear to ensure its longevity and effectiveness.

SWIMSUITS: COMPETITIVE VS. RECREATIONAL

Swimsuits are a fundamental piece of equipment for swimmers, designed to enhance performance and comfort in the water. The type of swimsuit you choose depends on whether you are swimming competitively or recreationally.

Competitive Swimsuits

- **Material and Design:** Competitive swimsuits are crafted from advanced materials like polyester, spandex, or a blend of both. These materials are designed to offer minimal drag and maximum flexibility. The construction often includes features such as compression technology to support muscles, reduce fatigue, and streamline the swimmer's body for better hydrodynamics.

- **Types:** For competitive swimming, there are several types of swimsuits, including:
  - *Tech Suits:* High-performance suits designed for racing. They are typically made from hydrophobic materials that repel water and enhance speed. Tech suits often have a sleek, tight-fitting design and may include additional features like bonded seams and strategic compression.

Competitive Swimsuit from the 1920s

Tech Suit

  - *Training Suits:* Used for daily practice, training suits are less specialized than tech suits but are still made from durable materials that withstand regular use. They offer comfort and freedom of movement.

- **Fit and Sizing:** A proper fit is crucial for competitive swimsuits. They should be snug but not restrictive, providing a streamlined shape while allowing full range of motion. Swimmers often need to try on several sizes to find the optimal fit for their body type.

Recreational Swimsuits

Training Suit

- **Material and Design:** Recreational swimsuits are made from more flexible and comfortable materials, such as nylon and spandex blends. They are designed for comfort rather than performance and come in a variety of styles, including one-piece suits, bikinis, and swim trunks.
- **Features:** Recreational swimsuits often feature additional elements like adjustable straps, built-in support, and more relaxed fits. They are designed for casual swimming, beach outings, and poolside relaxation.
- **Fit and Sizing:** For recreational swimsuits, comfort is the primary concern. The fit should be comfortable and allow for ease of movement. Unlike competitive swimsuits, recreational suits do not need to be as form-fitting or streamlined.

GOGGLES, SWIM CAPS, AND OTHER ACCESSORIES

Goggles

- **Purpose and Benefits:** Goggles are essential for protecting the eyes from chlorine and other pool chemicals. They also improve visibility underwater, allowing swimmers to see clearly and swim more efficiently.
- **Types:** There are various types of goggles designed for different purposes:
  - *Training Goggles:* Designed for everyday use, training goggles offer comfort and durability. They usually have adjustable straps and interchangeable lenses.

Training Goggles

  - *Competition Goggles:* These are streamlined for performance, with a low-profile design that reduces drag. They often come with features like anti-fog coating and tinted lenses for enhanced visibility in different lighting conditions.

ESSENTIAL GEAR AND EQUIPMENT

Competition Goggles

- **Fit and Adjustment:** Proper fit is crucial for goggles. They should create a seal around the eyes without causing discomfort. Most goggles come with adjustable straps and nose bridges to ensure a secure fit.

SWIM CAPS

Swim Cap

- **Purpose and Benefits:** Swim caps help reduce drag by streamlining the swimmer's profile and keeping hair out of the face. They also protect hair from chlorine damage.
- **Materials:** Swim caps are typically made from silicone, latex, or Lycra. Silicone caps are durable and provide a snug fit, while latex caps are more affordable and offer a snug, but less durable, fit. Lycra caps are comfortable but provide less drag reduction.
- **Choosing a Cap:** For competitive swimmers, silicone caps are often preferred due to their hydrodynamic properties and durability. Recreational swimmers may opt for more comfortable options like Lycra.

OTHER ACCESSORIES

- **Ear Plugs and Nose Clips:** Ear plugs help prevent water from entering the ears, which can be beneficial for swimmers who are prone to ear infections. Nose clips prevent water from entering the nose and are used primarily in competitive swimming.

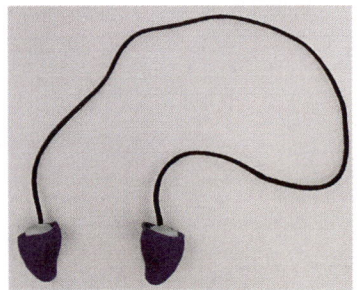

Ear Plugs   Nose Clip

- **Training Tools:** Various training tools can enhance swimming practice:
  - *Kickboards*: Used to isolate the legs during training, kickboards help swimmers focus on improving their kick technique and build leg strength.
  - *Pull Buoys*: Placed between the legs to keep the body in a streamlined position, pull buoys are used to focus on arm strokes and upper body strength.

  Swimming Kickboard

  Pull Buoy

  - *Fins and Paddles*: Fins provide propulsion and help improve kick technique, while paddles increase resistance and strengthen the upper body.

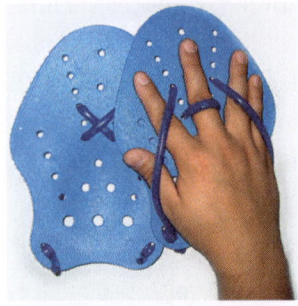
Hand Paddle

Fins

CARING FOR YOUR GEAR

Proper care and maintenance of swimming gear are essential for ensuring its longevity and effectiveness. Regular cleaning and proper storage help prevent wear and tear and maintain the performance of your equipment.

Swimsuits

- **Washing:** Rinse swimsuits with fresh water immediately after use to remove chlorine and salt. Hand wash with mild detergent and avoid using fabric softeners, which can damage the material. Air dry swimsuits away from direct sunlight and heat sources.
- **Storage:** Store swimsuits in a cool, dry place. Avoid folding or wringing the material, as this can cause deformation.

Goggles

- **Cleaning:** Rinse goggles with fresh water after each use to remove chlorine and debris. Clean the lenses with a

ESSENTIAL GEAR AND EQUIPMENT

soft cloth to prevent scratches.
- **Storage:** Store goggles in a protective case to prevent damage. Avoid leaving them in direct sunlight or extreme temperatures.

Swim Caps

- **Cleaning:** Rinse swim caps with fresh water after each use and allow them to air dry. Avoid folding or crumpling the caps, as this can cause damage.
- **Storage:** Store swim caps in a cool, dry place. Avoid exposure to chlorine and sunlight, which can degrade the material.

Training Tools

- **Kickboards and Pull Buoys:** Rinse with fresh water after each use to remove chlorine. Allow them to air dry before storing.
- **Fins and Paddles:** Rinse fins and paddles with fresh water to remove chlorine and debris. Store them in a cool, dry place and avoid direct sunlight.

Selecting the right gear and equipment for swimming enhances performance and enjoyment in the water.

4

THE BASICS OF WATER SAFETY

WATER SAFETY IS CRUCIAL FOR ANYONE involved in swimming, whether recreationally or competitively. Understanding the risks associated with water activities, learning essential survival skills, recognizing the role of lifeguards and swimming instructors, and knowing how to respond to emergencies are fundamental aspects of ensuring a safe and enjoyable experience in and around water. This chapter delves into these key elements of water safety, providing a comprehensive guide to navigating the aquatic environment safely.

UNDERSTANDING WATER SAFETY: RISKS AND PRECAUTIONS

Water safety encompasses various measures and precautions designed to prevent accidents and ensure the well-being of individuals in and around water. Recognizing the potential risks and implementing safety strategies are essential for preventing drowning and other water-related incidents.

Potential Risks

- **Drowning:** One of the most severe risks associated with water activities is drowning. It can occur quickly and silently, often within seconds. Drowning risks are higher in open water environments such as lakes, rivers, and oceans due to factors like currents, waves, and water temperature.
- **Waterborne Illnesses:** Swimming in contaminated water can lead to waterborne illnesses, including gastrointestinal infections and skin rashes. Proper hygiene, including showering before entering the pool, can help reduce the risk.
- **Injuries:** Injuries such as slips, trips, and falls around pool areas are common. Additionally, accidents resulting from collisions or improper use of pool equipment can occur.

Precautions

- **Supervision:** Always swim in the presence of a responsible adult, especially when children or inexperienced swimmers are involved. Continuous supervision is crucial for ensuring safety and providing immediate assistance if needed.
- **Swim with a Buddy:** Swimming with a partner or in groups can enhance safety. Buddies can assist each other in case of emergencies and provide immediate support if someone is struggling.
- **Understand Water Conditions:** Before entering any body of water, be aware of the conditions, including water temperature, current strength, and weather

conditions. Avoid swimming in severe weather or high surf conditions.
- **Follow Pool Rules:** Adhere to posted pool rules and guidelines. These rules are designed to ensure safety and prevent accidents.

Pool Rules

BASIC WATER SURVIVAL SKILLS

Developing essential water survival skills can significantly improve your ability to respond to emergencies and increase your overall safety in the water.

Floating and Treading Water

- **Floating:** Floating on your back or stomach helps conserve energy and provides a means of resting if you become tired. To float, lie on your back with your arms and legs spread out. Keep your head tilted back and maintain a calm, relaxed position.
- **Treading Water:** Treading water involves a vertical position where you use a combination of arm and leg movements to stay afloat. This skill is crucial for maintaining your position in the water without expending excessive energy.

Basic Swim Strokes

- **Freestyle (Front Crawl):** The freestyle stroke is the fastest and most common. It involves alternating arm movements and a flutter kick. Mastering this stroke improves your ability to cover distances quickly and efficiently.
- **Backstroke:** Swimming on your back, using alternating arm movements and a flutter kick, provides a comfortable and energy-efficient way to move through the water.
- **Breaststroke:** Characterized by simultaneous arm movements and a frog-like kick, the breaststroke is useful for maintaining a steady pace and conserving energy.
- **Butterfly:** The butterfly stroke involves simultaneous arm movements and a dolphin kick. While more challenging, it provides an effective full-body workout.

Safe Entry and Exit Techniques

- **Entering the Water:** When entering the water from the poolside, use the ladder or steps to avoid slips and falls. If entering from a diving board or platform, ensure that the area below is clear of other swimmers.
- **Exiting the Water:** To exit the pool, use the ladder or steps. Avoid climbing out of the pool using the side walls, as this can lead to slips or falls.

THE ROLE OF LIFEGUARDS AND SWIMMING INSTRUCTORS

Lifeguards and swimming instructors play a vital role in maintaining water safety and ensuring that swimmers adhere to safety protocols.

Lifeguard

- **Responsibilities:** Lifeguards are trained to prevent and respond to emergencies in aquatic environments. Their duties include monitoring swimmers, enforcing

pool rules, and providing first aid and rescue services when needed.
- **Training:** Lifeguards undergo rigorous training in water rescue techniques, first aid, CPR, and emergency response procedures. They are also trained to recognize and address potential hazards before they escalate.
- **Certification:** Lifeguard certification is obtained through accredited organizations such as the American Red Cross or YMCA. This certification ensures that lifeguards possess the necessary skills and knowledge to perform their duties effectively.

Swimming Instructors

Swimming Instructor

- **Role:** Swimming instructors teach individuals of all ages how to swim, improve their techniques, and develop water safety skills. They provide instruction in various strokes, safety practices, and basic survival skills.
- **Training:** Instructors are trained in swim technique instruction, water safety, and emergency response. They

may also hold certifications in CPR and first aid.
- **Benefits:** Working with a qualified instructor can enhance a swimmer's confidence, improve technique, and ensure that they acquire essential water safety skills.

HOW TO RESPOND TO WATER EMERGENCIES

Being prepared to respond effectively to water emergencies can save lives and minimize harm. Knowing how to act in emergencies ensures a swift and appropriate response.

Recognizing Emergencies

- **Signs of Distress:** Look for signs of distress in swimmers, such as flailing arms, struggling to stay afloat, or inability to call for help. Recognizing these signs early can prompt a timely response.
- **Drowning Indicators:** Drowning victims may not be able to call for help and may appear to be quietly struggling. Signs include a person's head low in the water, mouth at water level, and an inability to keep their head up.

Responding to Emergencies

- **Immediate Action:** If you see someone in distress, alert a lifeguard or call emergency services. If it is safe to do so, reach out to the person using a long object like a pole or throw them a flotation device.
- **Rescue Techniques:** Perform a rescue by extending a buoyant object or reaching from a safe distance. Avoid jumping into the water unless you are trained and equipped to handle the situation.

- **Providing First Aid:** After rescuing someone, check for breathing and a pulse. If the person is not breathing, perform CPR until help arrives. Use first aid techniques to address any injuries or medical conditions.

Preventing Future Incidents

- **Education:** Educate yourself and others about water safety practices, including the use of flotation devices and the importance of swimming in designated areas.
- **Regular Drills:** Participate in water safety drills and practice emergency response techniques to ensure readiness in case of real emergencies.

The basics of water safety is essential for preventing accidents and ensuring a safe experience in aquatic environments. By recognizing potential risks, developing essential survival skills, knowing the roles of lifeguards and swimming instructors, and learning how to respond to emergencies, swimmers can enhance their safety and enjoyment in the water. Emphasizing proactive safety measures and being prepared for emergencies helps create a safer aquatic environment for everyone.

SECTION TWO

LEARNING THE FUNDAMENTALS

5

GETTING COMFORTABLE IN THE WATER

GETTING COMFORTABLE IN THE WATER IS A CRUCIAL step for anyone learning to swim or aiming to improve their swimming skills. Overcoming fear, mastering basic floating techniques, learning effective breathing methods, and building confidence are foundational elements that contribute to a positive and successful swimming experience. This chapter explores these key aspects in detail to help swimmers develop comfort and proficiency in the water.

OVERCOMING FEAR OF WATER

Fear of water, also known as aquaphobia, is a common challenge for many individuals, whether beginners or those returning to swimming after a break. Addressing and overcoming this fear is essential for building confidence and enjoying the benefits of swimming.

Understanding Fear

- **Causes:** Fear of water can stem from various sources, including past traumatic experiences, lack of exposure to water, or anxiety about being in unfamiliar environments. It may also result from concerns about drowning or not being able to breathe underwater.
- **Psychological Impact:** Fear can cause physical and emotional responses such as rapid heartbeat, shallow breathing, and muscle tension. Understanding these reactions can help individuals address their fears more effectively.

Strategies for Overcoming Fear

- **Gradual Exposure:** Start by gradually exposing yourself to water in a controlled and safe environment. Begin with shallow water and slowly increase depth as comfort grows. This gradual approach helps desensitize the fear response and build familiarity.
- **Positive Reinforcement:** Celebrate small successes and progress. Recognize and reward yourself for each step taken towards overcoming fear. Positive reinforcement helps reinforce confidence and motivation.
- **Relaxation Techniques:** Practice relaxation techniques such as deep breathing, visualization, and progressive muscle relaxation to manage anxiety and promote calmness. These techniques can be used before and during water activities to reduce stress.
- **Professional Support:** Consider working with a swimming instructor or therapist specializing in water phobias. Professional guidance can provide personalized strategies and support tailored to individual needs.

BASIC FLOATING TECHNIQUES

Floating is a fundamental skill that helps swimmers feel more comfortable and confident in the water. It allows for relaxation, energy conservation, and improved overall body awareness.

Floating on the Back

- **Position:** To float on your back, lie flat in the water with your body extended. Keep your head tilted slightly back, eyes looking up, and face out of the water. Spread your arms and legs to create stability and balance.

Floating on the Back

- **Techniques:**
    - **Head Position**: Tilt your head back slightly to keep

GETTING COMFORTABLE IN THE WATER

your face out of the water. Avoid tucking your chin, as this can cause your body to sink.
- **Body Position:** Keep your body as horizontal as possible. Relax your muscles and let your body naturally float. Engage your core muscles to maintain stability.

Floating on the Stomach

- **Position:** To float on your stomach, extend your arms in front of you and spread your legs. Keep your face in the water with your head slightly raised to breathe.
- **Techniques:**
  - **Head Position**: Keep your face in the water, with your head aligned with your body. Lift your head slightly to breathe if needed.
  - **Body Position**: Maintain a streamlined position with a slight arch in your back. Relax your muscles and keep your movements gentle.

Floating on the Stomach

Using Floatation Devices

- **Types:** Floatation devices such as kickboards, noodles, and floatation belts can provide additional support and help build confidence. Use these devices initially to gain

comfort and gradually transition to floating without assistance.
- **Techniques:** Start with floatation devices in shallow water, practicing basic floating techniques. Gradually reduce reliance on devices as comfort and skill improve.

Floating Using a Floatation Device

Emphasizing gradual progress, setting achievable goals, and maintaining a supportive environment contribute to a successful and enjoyable swimming journey.

6

INTRODUCTION TO THE FOUR COMPETITIVE STROKES

COMPETITIVE SWIMMING CONSISTS OF FOUR primary strokes, each with its own unique techniques, benefits, and challenges. Understanding these strokes is essential for swimmers aiming to improve their performance, choose the right stroke for their strengths, and explore the complexities of medley swimming. This chapter provides a comprehensive introduction to the four competitive strokes: Freestyle, Backstroke, Breaststroke, and Butterfly, exploring their differences, advantages, and how to select the stroke that suits you best. Additionally, an overview of medley swimming introduces how these strokes are combined in competition.

OVERVIEW OF FREESTYLE, BACKSTROKE, BREASTSTROKE, AND BUTTERFLY

Freestyle (Front Crawl)

- **Description:** Freestyle, also known as the front crawl, is the fastest and most popular swimming stroke. It involves a face-down position with alternating arm movements and a flutter kick.

- **Technique:** The swimmer's arms move in a windmill motion, pulling the water to propel the body forward. The legs perform a flutter kick, providing balance and speed. The head is turned to the side to breathe, with one side of the face remaining in the water.
- **Benefits:** Freestyle is highly efficient for covering long distances quickly. It emphasizes cardiovascular endurance, muscular strength, and coordination.

Backstroke

- **Description:** Backstroke is the only competitive stroke performed on the back. It features alternating arm movements with a flutter kick, similar to freestyle but with the swimmer facing upward.
- **Technique:** The swimmer's arms move in a continuous, alternating motion, with each arm recovering above the water. The legs perform a flutter kick to maintain a streamlined position. Breathing is naturally facilitated as the face is above the water.
- **Benefits:** Backstroke enhances back and shoulder strength, improves posture, and provides a good alternative for swimmers who may struggle with face-down strokes. It is also beneficial for building endurance and core stability.

Breaststroke

- **Description:** Breaststroke is characterized by simultaneous arm movements and a frog-like kick. The

swimmer's chest remains close to the water surface, and the head is lifted to breathe.
- **Technique:** The arms move in a circular motion, pulling the water towards the body and then pushing it outward. The legs perform a frog kick, where the feet are drawn towards the body before kicking outward. Breathing is synchronized with the stroke, with the head lifting above the water during the arm pull phase.
- **Benefits:** Breaststroke is a slower stroke that emphasizes technique and coordination. It is effective for building upper body strength and is often used for longer distances due to its lower impact on the body.

Butterfly

- **Description:** Butterfly is known for its demanding technique and is characterized by simultaneous arm movements and a dolphin-like kick. It is one of the most challenging strokes to master.
- **Technique:** The arms move in a simultaneous, circular motion, pulling the water from the front to the back. The legs perform a dolphin kick, with both legs moving together in a fluid, undulating motion. Breathing occurs during the arm recovery phase, with the head lifting above the water.
- **Benefits:** Butterfly builds upper body and core strength, improves flexibility, and enhances overall swimming power. It requires coordination and rhythm, making it a valuable stroke for developing athleticism.

DIFFERENCES BETWEEN EACH STROKE

Each competitive stroke has distinct techniques, benefits, and applications. Understanding these differences is essential for swimmers to maximize their strengths and improve their overall performance.

Speed and Efficiency

- **Freestyle:** Known for its speed and efficiency, freestyle is the fastest stroke and is commonly used in sprint and distance events.
- **Backstroke:** While not as fast as freestyle, backstroke provides a more relaxed breathing pattern and is beneficial for swimmers who prefer an upright position.
- **Breaststroke:** This stroke is generally slower but emphasizes technique and endurance. It is often used in middle-distance events.
- **Butterfly:** Known for its power and speed, butterfly is challenging but effective for shorter distances and individual medley events.

Technique and Body Position

- **Freestyle:** Requires a horizontal body position and alternating arm movements with a flutter kick. Breathing is coordinated with arm strokes.
- **Backstroke:** Features an upright body position with alternating arm movements and a flutter kick. Breathing is continuous, with the face remaining above the water.
- **Breaststroke:** Involves a horizontal body position with simultaneous arm movements and a frog kick. Breathing is synchronized with the stroke, with the head lifting

above the water.
- **Butterfly:** Requires a horizontal body position with simultaneous arm movements and a dolphin kick. Breathing occurs during the arm recovery phase.

Training and Conditioning

- **Freestyle:** Emphasizes cardiovascular conditioning and endurance, with a focus on speed and efficiency.
- **Backstroke:** Enhances back and shoulder strength, with an emphasis on maintaining a streamlined position and continuous breathing.
- **Breaststroke:** Focuses on technique and coordination, with an emphasis on building upper body strength and endurance.
- **Butterfly:** Requires strength, power, and flexibility, with a focus on developing rhythm and coordination.

INTRODUCTION TO MEDLEY SWIMMING

Medley swimming involves combining all four competitive strokes in a single race. It is a challenging event that tests a swimmer's versatility, endurance, and technique across different strokes.

Individual Medley (IM)

- **Description:** In the Individual Medley, swimmers complete all four strokes in a specific order: Butterfly, Backstroke, Breaststroke, and Freestyle. Each segment requires precise transitions and techniques.
- **Technique:** Swimmers must master each stroke and practice smooth transitions between strokes. Efficient

transitions are crucial for maintaining speed and minimizing time losses.
- **Training:** Medley training involves focusing on each stroke separately and practicing transitions. Building endurance and mastering technique are key components of successful medley swimming.

Medley Relay

- **Description:** In the Medley Relay, teams of four swimmers each complete one of the four strokes in a relay format. Each swimmer swims a different stroke, and the team's overall time is recorded.
- **Technique:** Relay swimmers must execute efficient starts and transitions, and work together to ensure smooth exchanges between team members.
- **Training:** Medley relay training emphasizes teamwork, technique, and relay exchanges. Swimmers practice each stroke individually and work on seamless transitions during relay practice.

# SECTION THREE

MASTERING EACH STROKE

7

FREESTYLE (FRONT CRAWL)

F REESTYLE, OR FRONT CRAWL, IS THE FASTEST AND most versatile of the competitive swimming strokes. Its speed and efficiency make it a staple in swimming competitions and training regimes. This chapter delves into the intricate details of the freestyle stroke, including its mechanics, breathing techniques, methods for improving speed and efficiency, and common mistakes with their corrections.

MECHANICS OF THE FREESTYLE STROKE

Body Position

- **Horizontal Alignment:** Maintaining a horizontal body position is crucial for minimizing drag and maximizing propulsion. The swimmer's body should lie flat in the water, with a straight line from the head to the toes. The head should be in a neutral position, looking slightly forward and down. This alignment reduces resistance

FREESTYLE (FRONT CRAWL)

and helps maintain streamlined motion through the water.

Freestyle Stroke – Horizontal Alignment

- **Hip Rotation:** Effective freestyle involves a subtle rotation of the hips, which should be aligned with the stroke. This rotation is achieved by engaging the core muscles and allowing the body to move smoothly from side to side. Proper hip rotation helps in engaging the back muscles, leading to a more powerful and efficient stroke. It also assists in maintaining balance and proper body alignment.

Freestyle Stroke – Hip Rotation

Arm Technique

- **Entry and Catch:** The arm entry phase is critical for initiating the stroke. Begin with the arm extended and

slightly angled outward as it enters the water in front of the shoulder. This positioning helps create a strong catch phase, where the hand and forearm move downward to grip the water. The catch should be firm but not rigid, allowing the swimmer to create maximum propulsion.
- **Pull Phase:** During the pull phase, the arm should follow a "S" shaped path, moving from a wide position in front of the body to a narrower position closer to the torso. The elbow should be kept higher than the hand throughout this phase to maximize the surface area engaging with the water. The pull should be powerful and deliberate, with the aim of moving as much water as possible to propel the swimmer forward.
- **Recovery:** The recovery phase involves lifting the arm out of the water and moving it forward to re-enter for the next stroke. The arm should be kept straight and relaxed, with a high elbow position to reduce drag and maintain a smooth, streamlined motion. The recovery should be quick and efficient, minimizing the time the arm spends in the air.

Leg Technique

- **Flutter Kick:** The flutter kick is a continuous, rapid kicking motion generated from the hips with a slight bend in the knees. The legs should remain close to the water's surface, and the kick should be steady and rhythmic. The flutter kick provides propulsion and helps maintain body position, contributing to the overall efficiency of the stroke.

FREESTYLE (FRONT CRAWL)

Swimmers Practicing Flutter Kicks

- **Body Position:** Proper leg positioning is essential for reducing drag and maintaining a streamlined body. The legs should be extended but not overly rigid, with the feet slightly pointed. Avoid excessive splashing or kicking too hard, as this can lead to increased drag and reduced efficiency.

Breathing and Coordination

- **Breathing Timing:** Effective breathing is integral to a successful freestyle stroke. The timing of breathing should be coordinated with the arm strokes. Inhale quickly and deeply as you turn your head to the side, ensuring that the face is partially out of the water. Exhale smoothly through the nose when the face is back in the water, avoiding any breath-holding or gasping.
- **Head Position:** The head should remain in a neutral position, with minimal movement. Turn the head to the side to breathe, keeping the head aligned with the body.

Avoid lifting the head excessively, as this can cause the hips to drop and increase drag.

Freestyle Stroke – Breathing and Head Position

BREATHING TECHNIQUES: BILATERAL BREATHING

What is Bilateral Breathing?

- **Definition:** Bilateral breathing refers to the practice of breathing alternately on both sides while swimming freestyle. Typically, swimmers use a pattern where they breathe every three strokes, alternating between the left and right sides.
- **Benefits:** Bilateral breathing promotes a balanced stroke, improves symmetry, and helps prevent muscle fatigue. It ensures that both sides of the body are equally engaged, which can prevent overuse injuries and

enhance overall stroke efficiency. It also helps swimmers adapt to different conditions, such as choppy water or varying pool environments.

Training Drills

- **Three-Three Drill:** The three-three drill involves swimming three strokes while breathing on one side, then three strokes on the other side. This drill helps develop balance and coordination in breathing and improves stroke symmetry.
- **Breathing Every Five Strokes:** Practice breathing every five strokes to build a more even and rhythmic breathing pattern. This drill helps enhance overall breathing efficiency and endurance.

COMMON MISTAKES AND CORRECTIONS

Head Position

- **Mistake:** Lifting the head too high during breathing can cause the hips to drop and increase drag, reducing overall efficiency.
- **Correction:** Maintain a neutral head position, with minimal movement. Turn the head just enough to breathe and keep the face in the water during the stroke phase. This position helps maintain proper body alignment and reduces drag.

Arm Technique

- **Mistake:** Overreaching or crossing the arms in front of the body can cause inefficient propulsion and increased drag.

- **Correction:** Focus on proper arm entry and alignment. Ensure that the arms are slightly wider than shoulder-width apart and avoid crossing them in front of the body. Practice a smooth and controlled arm movement to maximize propulsion and minimize resistance.

Kick Technique

- **Mistake:** An excessive or inefficient kick can lead to fatigue and decreased speed.
- **Correction:** Perform a steady and controlled flutter kick, generating propulsion from the hips with minimal splashing. Keep the legs close to the water's surface and maintain a consistent kick rhythm to complement the arm stroke.

Breathing

- **Mistake:** Gasping for air or holding the breath can disrupt the stroke and reduce efficiency.
- **Correction:** Practice smooth and rhythmic breathing, coordinating inhalation with the arm stroke. Exhale through the nose while the face is in the water, and inhale quickly and deeply when the head is turned. Develop a breathing pattern that maintains stroke rhythm and avoids disruptions.

Regular practice, combined with a focus on proper body alignment, arm and leg techniques, and effective breathing, will contribute to overall success in freestyle swimming.

8

BACKSTROKE

BACKSTROKE, KNOWN FOR ITS DISTINCTIVE FACE-UP position, is one of the four competitive swimming strokes. It combines a unique set of mechanics and techniques that are crucial for efficient swimming and competitive performance. This chapter provides an in-depth look at the mechanics of the backstroke, including head position, body rotation, streamlining, turns, and common mistakes with their corrections.

MECHANICS OF THE BACKSTROKE

Body Position

- **Horizontal Alignment:** Maintaining a horizontal position in the water is essential for backstroke efficiency. The body should lie flat with a slight tilt to ensure that the head, shoulders, hips, and legs remain aligned. The waterline should be just below the ears, and the head should be in a neutral, relaxed position.

- **Hip Position:** The hips should be high in the water to reduce drag and maintain a streamlined profile. Proper hip alignment helps in balancing the stroke and ensures a more efficient propulsion through the water.

Backstroke – Horizontal Alignment and Hip Position

Arm Technique

- **Entry and Recovery:** The arm should enter the water with the pinky finger first, slightly angled outward. The arm entry should be in line with the shoulder to minimize resistance. The recovery phase involves lifting the arm out of the water, keeping it straight and relaxed. The arm should move in a circular motion, re-entering the water with the pinky finger first.
- **Pull Phase:** During the pull phase, the hand should move downward and outward, creating a catch to pull as much water as possible. The elbow should be slightly bent and higher than the hand to maximize the effectiveness of the pull. The pull should be smooth and powerful, with a continuous motion that propels the swimmer forward.
- **Arm Rotation:** Efficient backstroke involves a consistent

rotation of the arms. The rotation should be smooth, with the arms moving in a circular motion that helps maintain balance and streamline the stroke.

Leg Technique

- **Flutter Kick:** The flutter kick is similar to the freestyle kick, involving a continuous, rapid movement generated from the hips. The legs should remain close to the water's surface, with a slight bend in the knees. The kick should be steady and rhythmic, providing propulsion and helping maintain body position.
- **Body Alignment:** Proper leg positioning is crucial for reducing drag. The legs should be fully extended but not overly rigid. The feet should be slightly pointed, and the kick should be synchronized with the arm stroke to enhance efficiency.

HEAD POSITION AND BODY ROTATION

Head Position

- **Neutral Head Alignment:** The head should be in a neutral position, looking straight up towards the ceiling or sky. This position helps maintain a streamlined body profile and reduces drag. The head should not be lifted excessively, as this can cause the hips to drop and increase resistance.
- **Breathing:** In backstroke, breathing is continuous and natural. Since the face is always out of the water, swimmers can breathe freely without needing to coordinate breathing with the stroke. However, it's

important to maintain a consistent rhythm and avoid overexertion.

Body Rotation

- **Rotation Technique:** Effective backstroke involves a subtle rotation of the body from side to side with each stroke. This rotation helps engage the core muscles and facilitates a more powerful and efficient pull. The rotation should be smooth and rhythmic, with the shoulders and hips moving in sync.
- **Core Engagement:** Engaging the core muscles is crucial for maintaining proper body alignment and rotation. A strong core helps stabilize the body and prevents excessive rolling, which can disrupt the stroke and reduce efficiency.

STREAMLINING AND TURNS

Streamlining

- **Position and Form:** Streamlining in backstroke involves maintaining a streamlined body position with minimal resistance. The swimmer should focus on keeping the body flat and aligned, with the hips high and the legs close to the water's surface.
- **Arm Position:** The arms should be extended and positioned in a streamlined manner, with the hands close together. This position reduces drag and helps the swimmer move efficiently through the water.

Turns

- **Backstroke Flip Turn:** The backstroke flip turn involves rotating from the back onto the stomach, performing a somersault, and pushing off from the wall to resume the backstroke. The turn should be smooth and well-coordinated to maintain momentum and reduce time spent at the wall.
- **Execution:** Approach the wall with a steady rhythm, perform the flip turn by rotating onto the stomach, and complete the somersault while keeping the body streamlined. Push off from the wall with a strong kick, and transition smoothly back into the backstroke.

COMMON MISTAKES AND CORRECTIONS

Head Position

- **Mistake:** Lifting the head too high during the stroke can cause the hips to drop, increasing drag and reducing efficiency.
- **Correction:** Keep the head in a neutral position, looking straight up. Maintain a relaxed head position and avoid lifting it excessively. This helps maintain proper body alignment and reduces resistance.

Arm Technique

- **Mistake:** Overreaching or crossing the arms in front of the body can lead to inefficient propulsion and increased drag.
- **Correction:** Focus on proper arm entry and recovery, keeping the arms slightly wider than shoulder-width apart. Avoid crossing the arms and ensure a smooth,

circular motion to maximize propulsion and reduce resistance.

Leg Technique

- **Mistake:** Kicking too hard or inconsistently can lead to fatigue and reduced speed.
- **Correction:** Perform a steady and controlled flutter kick, focusing on generating propulsion from the hips. Maintain a rhythmic kick with minimal splashing to complement the arm stroke and enhance efficiency.

Body Rotation

- **Mistake:** Excessive rolling of the body can disrupt the stroke and reduce overall efficiency.
- **Correction:** Practice a smooth and consistent rotation, engaging the core muscles to maintain balance. Avoid excessive rolling and focus on keeping the shoulders and hips moving in sync.

Mastering backstroke involves a thorough understanding of its mechanics, including body position, arm and leg techniques, and effective streamlining. Addressing common mistakes and implementing targeted training drills will help swimmers improve their technique, enhance performance, and achieve competitive success. Regular practice, combined with a focus on proper body alignment, rotation, and turns, will contribute to overall proficiency in backstroke swimming.

9

BREASTSTROKE

BREASTSTROKE IS ONE OF THE MOST RECOGNIZABLE and strategic swimming strokes, known for its unique arm and leg movements and the distinctive frog-like kick. This chapter explores the mechanics of the breaststroke, focusing on timing, coordination, gliding, efficiency, and common mistakes with their corrections.

MECHANICS OF THE BREASTSTROKE

Body Position

- **Horizontal Alignment:** Maintaining a horizontal body position is essential for effective breaststroke swimming. The body should be flat in the water, with the chest slightly elevated to reduce drag. The head should be in a neutral position, looking slightly forward and down. This alignment helps streamline the swimmer's profile and enhances overall efficiency.
- **Head Position:** The head should be lifted just enough to allow the swimmer to breathe. Avoid excessive head

movement, as this can disrupt the stroke and increase resistance. When the head is out of the water, the gaze should be forward and slightly downward, aligning with the body to maintain a streamlined position.

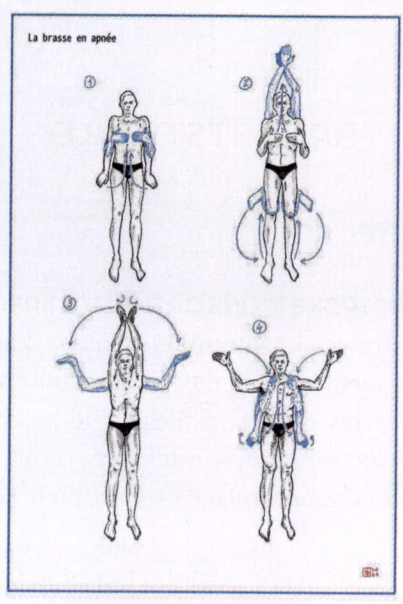

Breaststroke – Technique

Arm Technique

- **Arm Stroke:** The arm stroke in breaststroke consists of three main phases: the pull, the insweep, and the recovery.
    - *Pull Phase:* Begin with the arms extended in front of the body, palms facing outward. As the arms move outward and downward, they should form a "catch" position by creating an "S" shape in the water. This

motion engages the large muscle groups in the back and shoulders, providing powerful propulsion.
- *Insweep Phase:* After the pull, the arms should sweep inward, bending the elbows and bringing the hands toward the chest. This phase maximizes the amount of water pulled and increases propulsion. The hands should be turned slightly outward to enhance the effectiveness of the insweep.
- *Recovery Phase:* During the recovery, the arms should be brought back to the starting position, with the elbows slightly bent and close to the body. The hands should be relaxed and the motion should be smooth to prepare for the next stroke. The recovery phase should be quick but controlled, allowing for efficient transition between strokes.

Leg Technique

- **Frog Kick:** The frog kick is a key component of breaststroke, involving a distinctive, circular movement of the legs.
  - *Kick Phase:* Begin by bending the knees and bringing the feet towards the buttocks. As the legs are drawn in, they should be turned outward to prepare for the kick. The feet should be flexed and the ankles should be slightly bent.
  - *Power Phase:* As the legs are extended outward, perform a powerful kick by pushing against the water. The movement should be smooth and continuous, with the feet moving in a circular motion. The kick should be strong enough to provide propulsion while maintaining a streamlined body position.

- *Recovery Phase:* During the recovery phase, the legs should be brought back together in a controlled motion. The feet should be close to the surface, and the legs should be extended but relaxed. Avoid excessive splashing or kicking too hard, as this can increase drag and reduce efficiency.

Breathing

- **Breathing Technique:** In breaststroke, breathing is coordinated with the arm and leg strokes. Inhale quickly and deeply as the arms move through the pull and insweep phases, lifting the head slightly out of the water. Exhale smoothly through the nose as the face returns to the water during the recovery phase. The breathing pattern should be rhythmic and synchronized with the stroke.

TIMING AND COORDINATION

Stroke Timing

- **Stroke Coordination:** Effective breaststroke timing involves coordinating the arm stroke, leg kick, and breathing to maximize efficiency and speed. The stroke should be executed in a continuous, fluid motion, with each phase flowing seamlessly into the next. Proper timing ensures that the swimmer maintains a steady rhythm and minimizes resistance.
- **Timing Sequence:** The timing sequence for breaststroke involves the following pattern: arm pull, leg kick, glide, and recovery. The arms should complete their stroke before the legs kick, and the kick should be followed by a brief glide to maximize propulsion. Synchronize the

breathing with the arm stroke to ensure a smooth and efficient stroke.

Coordination Drills

- **Three-Three-Three Drill:** This drill involves performing three strokes of breaststroke with the arms only, followed by three strokes with the legs only, and then three strokes using the full stroke. This exercise helps develop coordination and timing by isolating each component of the stroke.
- **Single Arm Breaststroke:** Practice breaststroke using one arm at a time while keeping the other arm extended in front of the body. This drill helps improve arm technique and coordination by allowing swimmers to focus on the effectiveness of each arm stroke.

COMMON MISTAKES AND CORRECTIONS

Head Position

- **Mistake:** Lifting the head too high during the stroke can cause the hips to drop, increasing drag and reducing efficiency.
- **Correction:** Keep the head in a neutral position, with the eyes looking forward and slightly downward. Lift the head just enough to breathe, and maintain a streamlined body position to reduce resistance.

Arm Technique

- **Mistake:** Overreaching or crossing the arms in front of the body can lead to inefficient propulsion and increased drag.
- **Correction:** Focus on proper arm entry and recovery, with

the arms moving in a smooth, circular motion. Ensure that the arms are positioned slightly wider than shoulder-width apart and avoid crossing them in front of the body.

Leg Technique

- **Mistake:** Kicking too hard or inconsistently can lead to fatigue and decreased speed.
- **Correction:** Perform a steady and controlled frog kick, generating propulsion from the legs with minimal splashing. Maintain a rhythmic kick and ensure that the feet are turned outward to maximize efficiency.

Breathing

- **Mistake:** Gasps or holding the breath can disrupt the stroke and reduce overall efficiency.
- **Correction:** Practice smooth and rhythmic breathing, coordinating inhalation with the arm stroke. Exhale through the nose while the face is in the water, and inhale quickly and deeply when the head is lifted. Develop a breathing pattern that maintains stroke rhythm and avoids disruptions.

Mastering the breaststroke involves a comprehensive understanding of its mechanics, including body position, arm and leg techniques, timing, and gliding. Addressing common mistakes and implementing targeted training drills will help swimmers refine their technique, enhance performance, and achieve competitive success. Regular practice, combined with a focus on proper body alignment, timing, and efficiency, will contribute to overall proficiency in breaststroke swimming.

10

BUTTERFLY

THE BUTTERFLY STROKE, OFTEN REGARDED AS ONE of the most challenging and powerful strokes in competitive swimming, demands a combination of technique, strength, and rhythm. This chapter provides a comprehensive guide to mastering the butterfly stroke, covering its mechanics, the importance of rhythm and timing, developing power and endurance, and addressing common mistakes with their corrections.

MECHANICS OF THE BUTTERFLY STROKE

Body Position

- **Horizontal Alignment:** To execute the butterfly stroke effectively, maintaining a streamlined, horizontal body position is crucial. The body should be flat in the water, with a slight undulation as the chest and hips rise and fall. This motion helps reduce drag and increases propulsion.

- **Head Position:** The head should be in a neutral position, with the face looking forward and slightly downward. The head should be lifted just enough to breathe during the stroke, without disrupting the body's alignment. Proper head positioning helps maintain balance and streamline.

Arm Technique

- **Arm Pull:** The arm pull in butterfly involves a simultaneous, circular movement of both arms.
  - *Entry*: The hands should enter the water shoulder-width apart, with a slight angle to minimize resistance. The fingers should be pointed downward to create a strong catch.

Butterfly Stroke – Head, Body and Arm Position

  - *Pull Phase*: After entry, the arms should sweep outward and downward, creating a broad "catch" in the water. The elbows should be slightly bent and higher than the hands. The pull phase involves a powerful, continuous motion that engages the chest and shoulders.

o *Recovery Phase*: During the recovery, the arms should move out of the water in a relaxed, circular motion. The arms should be straight and close together, with a focus on smooth and efficient movement. The hands should re-enter the water with the pinky fingers first to prepare for the next stroke.

Leg Technique

- **Dolphin Kick:** The dolphin kick is a key component of the butterfly stroke, involving a powerful, undulating motion generated from the hips.
  - *Kick Phase:* Begin by bending the knees slightly and bringing the feet towards the buttocks. As the legs are extended, perform a powerful kick by pushing against the water. The kick should be fluid and rhythmic, with minimal splashing.

Dolphin Kick by Michael Phelps

  - *Undulation:* The dolphin kick involves a wave-like motion, starting from the hips and flowing through the legs. The movement should be smooth and continuous, with the feet moving in a coordinated pattern to provide propulsion.

Breathing

- **Breathing Technique:** In butterfly, breathing is synchronized with the arm stroke. Inhale quickly and deeply as the arms move through the pull phase and the head lifts out of the water. Exhale smoothly through the nose as the face returns to the water during the recovery phase. The breathing pattern should be rhythmic and coordinated with the stroke.

DEVELOPING POWER AND ENDURANCE

Building Power

- **Strength Training:** Incorporate strength training exercises to build power and endurance for the butterfly stroke. Focus on exercises that target the shoulders, chest, and core muscles. Examples include push-ups, shoulder presses, and core stability exercises.
- **Power Drills:** Perform drills that emphasize powerful arm pulls and kicks. Examples include fast butterfly sets, resistance band training, and explosive starts. These drills help develop the strength and power needed for competitive performance.

Endurance Training

- **Interval Training:** Incorporate interval training into your workout routine to build endurance for the butterfly stroke. Perform sets of butterfly with varying intervals of rest and work to improve stamina and overall performance.

Endurance Drills

- **Broken 200s:** Swim 200 meters of butterfly with breaks in between, such as 50 meters of easy swimming followed by a sprint. This drill helps build endurance and improve pacing.
- **Hypoxic Training:** Practice butterfly sets with limited breathing to improve lung capacity and breathing efficiency. For example, perform 25 meters of butterfly with every fourth stroke breathing.

COMMON MISTAKES AND CORRECTIONS

Head Position

- **Mistake:** Lifting the head too high during the stroke can cause the hips to drop and increase drag.
- **Correction:** Maintain a neutral head position, with the face looking slightly forward and downward. Lift the head just enough to breathe, and focus on keeping the body aligned and streamlined.

Arm Technique

- **Mistake:** Overreaching or crossing the arms can lead to inefficient propulsion and increased drag.
- **Correction:** Focus on proper arm entry and recovery, with the arms moving in a smooth, circular motion. Ensure that the arms are extended and close together during the recovery phase to maximize efficiency.

Leg Technique

- **Mistake:** Kicking too hard or inconsistently can lead to fatigue and reduced speed.
- **Correction:** Perform a steady and controlled dolphin kick, focusing on the undulating motion from the hips. Avoid excessive splashing and ensure that the kick is rhythmic and coordinated with the arm stroke.

Breathing

- **Mistake:** Holding the breath or gasping can disrupt the stroke and reduce overall efficiency.
- **Correction:** Practice smooth and rhythmic breathing, coordinating inhalation with the arm stroke. Exhale through the nose while the face is in the water, and inhale quickly and deeply when the head is lifted.

Regular practice, combined with a focus on maintaining proper body alignment, rhythm, and efficiency, will contribute to overall proficiency in butterfly swimming.

SECTION FOUR

ADVANCED TECHNIQUES AND TRAINING

11

STARTS, TURNS, AND FINISHES

IN COMPETITIVE SWIMMING, THE EXECUTION OF STARTS, turns, and finishes can significantly impact overall performance and race outcomes. This chapter explores the importance of a strong start, mastering flip turns and open turns, finishing techniques for different strokes, and drills to enhance these critical aspects of swimming.

THE IMPORTANCE OF A STRONG START

Why Starts Matter

- **Impact on Race Performance:** The start sets the tone for the entire race, often determining the swimmer's position relative to competitors. A strong, explosive start allows swimmers to gain a quick advantage and establish their pace early on. The speed and efficiency of the start can influence the swimmer's momentum and energy levels throughout the race.

- **Efficiency and Speed:** A well-executed start minimizes drag and maximizes propulsion, providing a powerful launch off the blocks. Key components of a successful start include reaction time, explosive power, and streamlined entry into the water. Improving these elements can lead to faster overall times and enhanced race performance.

Start in a Swimming Competition

Components of a Strong Start

- **Pre-Start Preparation:** Effective starts begin with proper preparation. Swimmers should position themselves correctly on the starting blocks, with a balanced stance and an athletic posture. The body should be slightly crouched, with the feet firmly planted and the hands gripping the block.
- **Reaction Time:** The ability to react quickly to the starting signal is crucial for a strong start. Practice reaction time drills and focus on explosive power to

ensure a quick and efficient launch off the blocks.
- **Entry Technique:** The entry into the water should be streamlined and minimal in resistance. Aim for a clean, vertical entry with the body in a streamlined position. This reduces drag and allows for a smooth transition into the swimming stroke.

Start Drills

- **Block Starts:** Practice explosive starts from the blocks, focusing on a quick reaction and powerful push off. Perform multiple repetitions to develop muscle memory and improve reaction time.

Swimmers diving off starting blocks

- **Underwater Kicking:** After the start, practice underwater kicking to build strength and improve the transition from the start to the first stroke. Focus on maintaining a streamlined position and generating power with each kick.

STARTS, TURNS, AND FINISHES

Underwater Kicking

MASTERING FLIP TURNS AND OPEN TURNS

Flip Turns

- **Execution:** Flip turns are used in freestyle and butterfly events to quickly change direction at the wall. The turn involves a somersault in the water, followed by a push off the wall and a streamlined transition into the next length.
- **Technique:** Approach the wall with speed and initiate the turn by tucking the chin and performing a forward roll. As the body completes the flip, prepare for a powerful push off the wall with the feet. Ensure that the body remains streamlined and aligned for a smooth transition.
- **Drills:** Practice flip turns with specific drills, such as the "flip turn drill" where swimmers perform multiple turns in succession, focusing on smooth execution

and efficient transitions. Use video analysis to assess technique and make adjustments.

Open Turns

- **Execution:** Open turns are used in breaststroke and backstroke events, where a simpler, more controlled turn is required. The swimmer approaches the wall, executes a pivot or touch, and pushes off to continue the race.
- **Technique:** For breaststroke, approach the wall with a two-handed touch and a quick, controlled pivot. For backstroke, perform a quick touch and rotation to face the wall, then push off with the feet. Focus on maintaining speed and minimizing time spent at the wall.
- **Drills:** Practice open turns with drills that emphasize speed and efficiency. For example, perform sets of open turns with varying distances to improve technique and reduce time spent at the wall.

Turn Drills

- **Wall Touches:** Practice wall touches with a focus on proper technique and speed. Perform multiple repetitions of touch-and-go drills to improve turn efficiency and overall performance.
- *Turn Timing*: Incorporate drills that focus on the timing of turns within sets. For example, perform intervals with specific turn points to simulate race conditions and improve turn execution.

FINISHING TECHNIQUES FOR DIFFERENT STROKES

Freestyle and Butterfly

- **Approach:** In freestyle and butterfly, the final approach to the wall should be powerful and controlled. Maintain a strong kick and steady stroke rate to build momentum for the finish.
- **Touch:** For freestyle, perform a strong and controlled touch with one hand, ensuring that the body is fully extended and streamlined. For butterfly, execute a powerful two-handed touch, focusing on maintaining body position and momentum.

Backstroke

- **Approach:** In backstroke, the final approach involves a controlled entry into the wall. As the swimmer nears the wall, prepare for a quick and efficient touch or flip turn.
- **Touch:** Perform a precise backstroke touch by reaching out with both hands and ensuring that the body remains aligned. Focus on a strong push off the wall to maintain speed and momentum.

Breaststroke

- **Approach:** In breaststroke, the final approach involves a controlled and efficient touch. Approach the wall with a strong kick and smooth stroke rate to build momentum for the finish.
- **Touch:** Execute a two-handed touch with a focus on precision and control. Ensure that the body remains

streamlined and aligned, and prepare for a strong push off the wall.

Finishing Drills

- **Finish Touch Drill:** Practice finishing touches with a focus on precision and speed. Perform multiple repetitions of finish touches for each stroke, emphasizing strong and controlled execution.
- **Race Simulation:** Incorporate finishing techniques into race simulations to practice the final approach and touch. Perform sets of simulated races with a focus on maintaining speed and efficiency throughout the final length.

DRILLS TO IMPROVE STARTS, TURNS, AND FINISHES

Start Drills

- **Block Start Practice:** Perform repeated block starts to develop power and technique. Focus on explosive launches and streamlined entries to enhance overall performance.
- **Underwater Kicking Drills:** Incorporate underwater kicking drills into training to build strength and improve the transition from the start to the first stroke. Focus on maintaining a streamlined position and generating power with each kick.

Turn Drills

- **Flip Turn Drills:** Practice flip turns with a focus on smooth execution and efficient transitions. Perform multiple repetitions of flip turns, using video analysis to assess technique and make adjustments.
- **Open Turn Drills:** Practice open turns with specific drills that emphasize speed and efficiency. Perform sets of open turns with varying distances to improve technique and reduce time spent at the wall.

Finishing Drills

- **Finish Precision Drills:** Perform drills that focus on finishing touches for each stroke, emphasizing strong and controlled execution. Use race simulations to practice finishing techniques and improve overall performance.
- **Speed Endurance Sets:** Incorporate speed endurance sets into training to build strength and improve finishing techniques. Perform intervals with a focus on maintaining speed and efficiency throughout the final length.

Mastering starts, turns, and finishes is essential for optimizing performance in competitive swimming. By focusing on proper technique, rhythm, and timing, and incorporating targeted drills into training, swimmers can enhance their overall race performance and achieve competitive success. Regular practice and attention to detail in these critical areas will contribute to improved starts, turns, and finishes, ultimately leading to faster times and better race outcomes.

12

DEVELOPING ENDURANCE AND SPEED

To excel in competitive swimming, developing both endurance and speed is crucial. This chapter delves into the role of cardiovascular conditioning, the benefits of interval training, the balance between sprint and distance workouts, and strategies for monitoring progress and adjusting workouts to optimize performance.

THE ROLE OF CARDIOVASCULAR CONDITIONING

Cardiovascular Fitness

- **Importance:** Cardiovascular conditioning is the foundation of swimming endurance and overall performance. A well-developed cardiovascular system improves the efficiency of oxygen transport to muscles, enhances stamina, and supports sustained physical exertion.

- **Training Adaptations:** Regular cardiovascular training increases the heart's ability to pump blood more effectively, strengthens the lungs, and improves blood vessel elasticity. These adaptations result in better endurance, faster recovery, and enhanced performance in the pool.

Types of Cardiovascular Conditioning

- **Continuous Training:** This involves long, steady-state swims at a moderate intensity. Continuous training helps build aerobic capacity and endurance by challenging the cardiovascular system to sustain effort over extended periods.
- **Fartlek Training:** Fartlek, or "speed play," combines periods of high intensity with moderate or low-intensity recovery periods. This type of training improves both aerobic and anaerobic capacities, making it effective for swimmers looking to enhance endurance and speed simultaneously.
- **Long Swim Sets:** Incorporate long swim sets into training, focusing on maintaining a steady pace over longer distances. This builds endurance and prepares swimmers for the demands of competitive events.

INTERVAL TRAINING FOR SWIMMERS

What is Interval Training?

- **Definition:** Interval training involves alternating between periods of high-intensity effort and lower-intensity recovery. This approach enhances both

aerobic and anaerobic capacities by challenging the cardiovascular system with varied intensities.
- **Benefits:** Interval training improves speed, endurance, and lactate threshold. It also helps swimmers adapt to the demands of different race distances and paces, making it a versatile and effective training method.

Types of Interval Training

- **Short Intervals:** Short intervals involve brief, high-intensity efforts followed by short recovery periods. For example, swim 50 meters at maximum effort, followed by 30 seconds of rest. This type of interval training enhances speed and power.
- **Medium Intervals:** Medium intervals involve slightly longer efforts with moderate recovery periods. For example, swim 100 meters at a high intensity, followed by 60 seconds of rest. This type of interval training improves both endurance and speed.
- **Long Intervals:** Long intervals involve extended efforts with longer recovery periods. For example, swim 400 meters at a challenging pace, followed by 2 minutes of rest. This type of interval training builds endurance and enhances pacing strategies.

Designing an Interval Training Set

- **Intensity:** Determine the appropriate intensity for each interval based on the swimmer's goals and fitness level. Use heart rate monitors or perceived exertion scales to gauge effort.
- **Recovery:** Adjust recovery periods to match the intensity of the intervals. Shorter recoveries may be used

DEVELOPING ENDURANCE AND SPEED

for higher-intensity intervals, while longer recoveries may be needed for extended efforts.
- **Progression:** Gradually increase the intensity and duration of intervals over time to continue challenging the cardiovascular system and promoting improvement.

SPRINT WORKOUTS VS. DISTANCE WORKOUTS

Sprint Workouts

- **Focus:** Sprint workouts emphasize short, high-intensity efforts designed to develop explosive speed and power. These workouts involve maximal effort over short distances, with ample recovery to maintain high performance.
- **Benefits:** Sprint workouts improve acceleration, maximum speed, and anaerobic capacity. They also enhance the swimmer's ability to sustain high-intensity efforts and recover quickly between sprints.
- **Examples:** Perform sets of 25 or 50 meters at maximum effort, with sufficient rest between sprints. Incorporate various sprint drills, such as starts and underwater kicks, to target different aspects of speed and power.

Distance Workouts

- **Focus:** Distance workouts focus on longer, steady-state efforts to build aerobic endurance and stamina. These workouts involve sustained effort over extended distances, with a focus on pacing and technique.
- **Benefits:** Distance workouts improve cardiovascular conditioning, muscular endurance, and pacing strategies.

They also enhance the swimmer's ability to maintain consistent performance throughout longer races.
- **Examples:** Swim sets of 800 to 1500 meters at a moderate intensity, with emphasis on maintaining a steady pace and proper technique. Incorporate long intervals and continuous swims to build endurance.

Balancing Sprint and Distance Workouts

- **Periodization:** Use periodization to balance sprint and distance workouts throughout the training cycle. Focus on sprint workouts during periods of high-intensity training and distance workouts during periods of aerobic base building.
- **Individual Needs:** Tailor workouts to the swimmer's specific goals and event distances. Sprinters may focus more on high-intensity intervals and sprint sets, while distance swimmers may emphasize longer, steady-state efforts.

Developing endurance and speed is essential for competitive swimming success. By incorporating effective cardiovascular conditioning, interval training, sprint and distance workouts, and systematic monitoring and adjustment, swimmers can enhance their performance and achieve their goals. Regular practice, combined with targeted training strategies, will lead to improved endurance, speed, and overall race performance.

13

STRENGTH TRAINING FOR SWIMMERS

STRENGTH TRAINING IS NOT MERELY AN ADJUNCT TO swimming but a foundational component that amplifies performance, refines technique, and mitigates the risk of injuries. This chapter delves deep into dryland exercises tailored for swimmers, the critical role of core training, flexibility and mobility routines, and comprehensive strategies for injury prevention and rehabilitation. Together, these elements form the backbone of a swimmer's off-water preparation, enabling them to excel in the pool.

DRYLAND EXERCISES TO BUILD STRENGTH

Purpose and Importance of Dryland Training

Dryland training is essential for swimmers, offering a pathway to develop the muscular strength and power required for faster and more efficient swimming. While swimming itself is a resistance exercise, it predominantly targets certain muscle groups. Dryland training complements this by engaging the entire body, especially focusing on areas that may not be as activated in the water but are crucial for overall swimming performance.

Key Dryland Exercises

- **Resistance Training:** Resistance exercises should be the cornerstone of a swimmer's dryland routine. They help in building the strength necessary for powerful strokes, starts, and turns. Exercises such as squats, deadlifts, and bench presses are vital.
  - *Squats and Deadlifts:* Squats build lower body strength, enhancing the power of kicks and starts. Deadlifts, on the other hand, target the posterior chain (hamstrings, glutes, and lower back), which is crucial for maintaining body position in the water.
  - *Bench Presses and Rows:* Upper body strength, particularly in the chest, shoulders, and back, is crucial for powerful strokes. Bench presses strengthen the pectoral muscles, while rows focus on the back muscles, both of which contribute to stronger pulls during freestyle, backstroke, and butterfly.
- **Plyometric Exercises:** Plyometrics focus on explosive power, crucial for quick starts and powerful turns. They train the fast-twitch muscle fibers responsible for sudden, forceful movements.
  - *Box Jumps:* Box jumps enhance explosive leg power, improving a swimmer's push-off from the blocks and turns. The emphasis should be on the height

and speed of each jump, with a focus on controlled landings to prevent injury.
  - *Medicine Ball Slams and Throws:* These exercises develop explosive upper body strength and improve coordination between the upper and lower body, which is essential for synchronized, powerful strokes.
- **Functional Training:** Functional exercises mimic the movements used in swimming and enhance overall body coordination and stability. These exercises improve the swimmer's ability to maintain proper technique and form during long races or intense training sessions.
  - *Stability Ball Rollouts:* This exercise targets the core and shoulder stability, critical for maintaining body alignment during strokes. By rolling the ball out while keeping the core tight, swimmers can improve the strength and endurance of the muscles that support efficient body positioning.
  - *Kettlebell Swings:* Kettlebell swings work on hip drive and core stability, which are essential for powerful starts and maintaining speed through the water. This exercise also promotes full-body coordination, crucial for effective and efficient swimming.

CORE TRAINING AND ITS IMPORTANCE IN SWIMMING

Why Core Strength is Essential

Core strength is central to a swimmer's ability to maintain streamline positions, transfer power from the lower to the upper body, and reduce drag in the water. A strong core allows swimmers to hold efficient body positions, especially during challenging parts of the race, such as turns and underwater phases. Additionally, core strength is key to preventing injuries, particularly in the lower back and shoulders, which are common among swimmers.

Core-Strengthening Exercises

- **Planks and Variations:** Planks are a simple yet effective way to build core strength. They engage the entire core, including the abdominals, obliques, and lower back, which are crucial for maintaining a stable and streamlined position in the water.

Standard Plank

- ○ *Standard Plank:* The standard plank focuses on maintaining a straight line from head to heels, engaging the core muscles to support the body.

Increasing hold times and adding variations, such as lifting one leg or arm, can intensify the exercise.
- *Side Plank:* Side planks specifically target the obliques, which are important for rotation during freestyle and backstroke. Alternating sides ensures balanced strength and prevents muscle imbalances that could lead to injury.

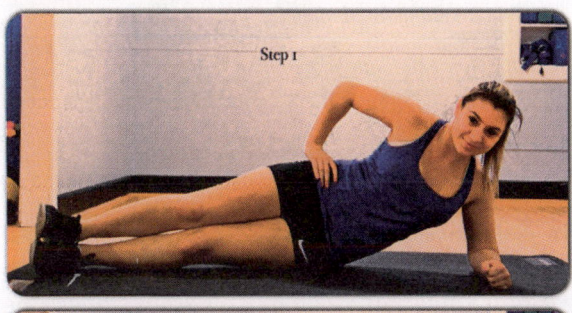

Side Plank

- **Russian Twists:** This exercise enhances rotational strength, which is vital for efficient stroke execution, especially in freestyle and backstroke. Holding a weight or medicine ball during the twists adds resistance, increasing the challenge and effectiveness.

Russian Twist

- **Leg Raises:** Leg raises are essential for strengthening the lower abdominals and hip flexors, muscles that are heavily involved in kicking. This exercise also helps in improving lower back strength, reducing the risk of injury during intensive training.

Leg Raises

- **Bicycle Crunches:** Bicycle crunches engage the entire core with a focus on the obliques, improving the rotational strength needed for powerful strokes. This exercise also enhances coordination between the upper and lower body, which is critical for efficient swimming.

Bicycle Crunch

14

NUTRITION, REST, AND INJURY PREVENTION FOR SWIMMERS

SWIMMING IS AN ENERGY-INTENSIVE SPORT THAT requires a well-balanced diet and effective recovery strategies to maintain peak performance and prevent injuries. Proper nutrition ensures that swimmers have the energy needed for prolonged training sessions and effective recovery, while adequate rest and injury prevention techniques are crucial for long-term success in the sport.

NUTRITION FOR OPTIMAL PERFORMANCE

Swimming demands high endurance, strength, and speed, all influenced by a swimmer's diet. The right nutrition provides the energy needed for both training and competition.

- **Energy Requirements & Macronutrient Balance:** Swimmers burn significant calories due to water resistance, which is 800 times denser than air. A diet rich in complex carbohydrates, lean proteins, and healthy

fats is essential. Carbohydrates fuel muscles during high-intensity workouts, proteins aid in muscle repair and growth, and healthy fats support energy levels and cell function.
- **Timing of Meals & Pre-Competition Nutrition:** Meal timing is crucial. A carbohydrate and protein-rich meal before training optimizes performance, while a post-workout protein-rich meal aids recovery. Before competitions, carb-loading maximizes glycogen stores for endurance events. A pre-race meal should be rich in easily digestible carbohydrates and moderate in protein.
- **Hydration & Supplements:** Hydration is vital, with swimmers needing consistent water intake throughout the day and during training. Supplements, such as protein powders, creatine, and omega-3 fatty acids, can enhance performance, but they should complement a balanced diet, not replace it.

RECOVERY AND INJURY PREVENTION

Rest and recovery are as important as the workout itself. They allow the body to repair, strengthen, and prepare for the next session, reducing the risk of overtraining, injury, and burnout.

- **Physical & Mental Recovery:** Rest is crucial for muscle repair (muscle protein synthesis) and mental rejuvenation. Quality sleep (7-9 hours per night) is essential for releasing growth hormones that aid in tissue repair and muscle growth.
- **Managing Muscle Soreness:** Light, low-intensity

activities, such as walking or swimming at a leisurely pace, can reduce muscle soreness. Proper hydration, nutrition, stretching, and foam rolling also play key roles in recovery.
- **Preventing Common Injuries:** The repetitive nature of swimming can lead to overuse injuries, particularly in the shoulders, knees, and lower back. Strengthening targeted muscle groups, maintaining proper stroke technique, and incorporating regular stretching can help prevent these injuries.
- **Recovery Techniques:** Massage therapy, ice baths, cryotherapy, compression garments, hydrotherapy, and active recovery sessions can all aid in reducing muscle tension, improving circulation, and promoting faster recovery.

By understanding the critical role of nutrition, recovery, and injury prevention, swimmers can enhance their performance, extend their competitive careers, and reach their full potential in the pool.

15

NURTURING A FUTURE OLYMPIC SWIMMER

BUILDING AN OLYMPIC SWIMMER REQUIRES A combination of early engagement, proper training, mental toughness, and a supportive environment. With the right foundation and consistent guidance, young athletes can be nurtured toward excellence in the sport of swimming.

EARLY EXPOSURE TO WATER

Start with Water Familiarity: Introduce young children to the water as early as possible to build comfort and confidence. Parent-child swim classes or splash time in shallow pools are excellent for developing early water skills.

Swimming Lessons: Enroll kids in swim classes that focus on teaching the four basic strokes—freestyle, backstroke, breaststroke, and butterfly. Learning these skills early builds a strong technical foundation.

FINDING THE RIGHT COACH AND SWIM CLUB

Selecting a Qualified Coach: A strong, experienced coach is essential for developing a young swimmer's potential. Look for someone with a background in competitive swimming and experience working with young athletes.

Joining a Competitive Swim Team: Once the basics are mastered, consider joining a local swim club. Clubs provide structured training, access to pools, and competitive opportunities. Ensure the club promotes a positive, disciplined environment.

PHYSICAL CONDITIONING AND TECHNIQUE MASTERY

Strength and Endurance: Swimming requires both cardiovascular endurance and muscle strength. Encourage participation in cross-training activities like running, cycling, or dryland strength exercises to build overall fitness.

Refining Technique: As young swimmers advance, the focus should be on refining their strokes. Good technique is critical to swimming efficiently and avoiding injury. Regular stroke drills and video analysis can help with correction.

Building Speed and Endurance: Introduce interval training to improve both speed and endurance in the water. Challenge swimmers with different distances and pacing to keep workouts varied and effective.

MENTAL TOUGHNESS AND DISCIPLINE

Developing Mental Strength: Olympic swimmers need mental toughness to handle long training sessions and the pressure of competition. Teach young swimmers to embrace challenges and setbacks as opportunities for growth.

Goal Setting: Help swimmers set clear, achievable goals for short-term and long-term success. Whether it's improving a personal best time or mastering a new stroke, goal-setting helps maintain focus and motivation.

Visualization and Focus: Encourage swimmers to visualize their races and practice mental focus. These techniques help young athletes prepare mentally for meets and stay calm under pressure.

THE PATH TO THE OLYMPICS

Dedication to Training: Olympic swimmers train for years, often logging thousands of hours in the pool. Encouraging dedication, even through tough phases, is key to long-term success.

Competitive Exposure: Competing in regional, national, and international meets is essential for young swimmers looking to qualify for the Olympics. Participation in higher-level competitions will help them gain experience and recognition.

Staying Focused: The journey to the Olympics is long and challenging. Maintaining a balance of hard work, passion, and resilience will keep swimmers on the path toward achieving their dreams.

16

FILIPINO OLYMPIANS IN SWIMMING: SPIRIT IN OLYMPIC WATERS

THE PHILIPPINES HAS A RICH SPORTING TRADITION, and while the country is more commonly known for its prowess in basketball and boxing, Filipino swimmers have made significant strides on the world stage, particularly in the Olympics. Though the Philippines has yet to secure an Olympic medal in swimming, the journey of its athletes reflects determination, passion, and an unyielding spirit. Let's explore the key figures who have represented the country in swimming and left a mark in Olympic history.

PIONEERS OF FILIPINO SWIMMING

Swimming has been part of the Philippines' Olympic journey since the early years of the modern Olympic Games. **Teofilo Yldefonso**, known as "The Ilocano Shark," remains one of the most celebrated athletes, not just in swimming but in all of Filipino sports. Though Yldefonso is famous for his achievements in the breaststroke, winning two Olympic

Teófilo Yldefonso

bronze medals in 1928 and 1932, his dedication inspired future generations of Filipino swimmers. His successes paved the way for the next wave of Filipino Olympians, even though Yldefonso himself competed in the breaststroke, which differs from the freestyle and butterfly strokes most commonly associated with Filipino swimming Olympians today.

Another early pioneer was **Jacinto Cayco**, who represented the Philippines in the 1956 Melbourne Olympics. While Cayco didn't win any medals, his participation marked the growing interest in competitive swimming in the country, inspiring younger athletes to aim for the international stage.

TRAILBLAZERS IN RECENT YEARS

The modern era of Filipino Olympic swimming saw a resurgence of talent in the late 20th and early 21st centuries. One of the most notable names in recent history is **Eric Buhain**, who represented the Philippines in the 1988 Seoul Olympics and again in the 1992 Barcelona Olympics. Known for his versatility in both butterfly and freestyle events, Buhain was a two-time Southeast Asian Games (SEA Games) gold medalist and set multiple national records during his career. Though he didn't secure an Olympic medal, his contribution to the sport laid the foundation for the future of Filipino swimming.

Eric Buhain

Another significant figure is **Raymond Papa**, who competed in the 1996 Atlanta Olympics. Specializing in the backstroke, Papa remains one of the most respected names in Filipino swimming. Though he didn't advance to the medal rounds, his Olympic journey raised the profile of swimming in the Philippines, motivating a new generation of swimmers to compete at the highest levels.

THE PRESENT GENERATION

In the 21st century, Filipino swimmers continue to strive for Olympic success, with athletes like **Jasmine Alkhaldi** and **Remedy Rule** representing the new generation of Filipino talent. Alkhaldi, who competed in the 2012 London Olympics and 2016 Rio Olympics, specializes in freestyle events and is a multi-time SEA Games medalist. Her perseverance and determination have earned her recognition as one of the Philippines' top female swimmers.

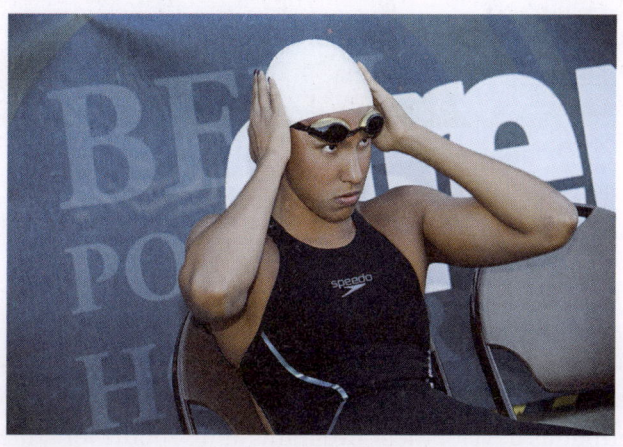

Jasmine Alkhaldi

Remedy Rule, another standout swimmer, made her Olympic debut in the 2020 Tokyo Olympics, competing in the butterfly events. Though she didn't advance to the finals, Rule's qualification alone was a significant achievement, as she represented a country with limited resources in terms of swimming infrastructure and development. Her presence on the Olympic stage is a testament to the dedication and hard work that Filipino swimmers bring to the sport.

Remedy Rule

THE FUTURE OF FILIPINO SWIMMING

While the dream of an Olympic swimming medal remains elusive, the future looks bright for Filipino swimmers. With continuous development programs and support for athletes, there is hope that the next generation will break through on the international stage. Jasmine Alkhaldi and Remedy Rule have already shown that Filipino swimmers can compete against the world's best, and their journeys will undoubtedly inspire others to follow in their footsteps.

LIST OF OLYMPIC MEDALISTS IN SWIMMING (2000-2024)

MEN

50 Metre Freestyle

Games	Gold		Silver		Bronze	
2000 Sydney	Anthony Ervin — United States Gary Hall Jr. — United States	21.98	*Not awarded* as there was a tie for gold.		Pieter van den Hoogenband — Netherlands	22.03
2004 Athens	Gary Hall Jr. — United States	21.93	Duje Draganja — Croatia	21.94	Roland Mark Schoeman — South Africa	22.02
2008 Beijing	César Cielo — Brazil	21.30 OR	Amaury Leveaux — France	21.45	Alain Bernard — France	21.49
2012 London	Florent Manaudou — France	21.34	Cullen Jones — United States	21.54	César Cielo — Brazil	21.59

Games	Gold		Silver		Bronze	
2016 Rio de Janeiro	Anthony Ervin 🇺🇸 United States	21.40	Florent Manaudou 🇫🇷 France	21.41	Nathan Adrian 🇺🇸 United States	21.49
2020 Tokyo	Caeleb Dressel 🇺🇸 United States	21.07 OR	Florent Manaudou 🇫🇷 France	21.55	Bruno Fratus 🇧🇷 Brazil	21.57
2024 Paris	Cameron McEvoy 🇦🇺 Australia	21.25	Benjamin Proud 🇬🇧 Great Britain	21.30	Florent Manaudou 🇫🇷 France	21.56

100 Metre Freestyle

Games	Gold		Silver		Bronze	
2000 Sydney	Pieter van den Hoogenband Netherlands	48.30 set WR in semifinal	Alexander Popov Russia	48.69	Gary Hall Jr. United States	48.73
2004 Athens	Pieter van den Hoogenband Netherlands	48.17	Roland Mark Schoeman South Africa	48.23	Ian Thorpe Australia	48.56
2008 Beijing	Alain Bernard France	47.21	Eamon Sullivan Australia	47.32 set WR in semifinal	Jason Lezak United States / César Cielo Brazil	47.67
2012 London	Nathan Adrian United States	47.52	James Magnussen Australia	47.53	Brent Hayden Canada	47.80
2016 Rio de Janeiro	Kyle Chalmers Australia	47.58	Pieter Timmers Belgium	47.80	Nathan Adrian United States	47.85
2020 Tokyo	Caeleb Dressel United States	47.02 OR	Kyle Chalmers Australia	47.08	Kliment Kolesnikov ROC	47.44
2024 Paris	Pan Zhanle China	46.40 WR	Kyle Chalmers Australia	47.48	David Popovici Romania	47.49

200 Metre Freestyle

Games	Gold		Silver		Bronze	
2000 Sydney	Pieter van den Hoogenband — Netherlands	1:45.35 WR	Ian Thorpe — Australia	1:45.83	Massimiliano Rosolino — Italy	1:46.65
2004 Athens	Ian Thorpe — Australia	1:44.71 OR	Pieter van den Hoogenband — Netherlands	1:45.23	Michael Phelps — United States	1:45.32
2008 Beijing	Michael Phelps — United States	1:42.96 WR	Park Tae-hwan — South Korea	1:44.85	Peter Vanderkaay — United States	1:45.14
2012 London	Yannick Agnel — France	1:43.14	Park Tae-hwan — South Korea Sun Yang — China	1:44.93	none awarded	
2016 Rio de Janeiro	Sun Yang — China	1:44.65	Chad le Clos — South Africa	1:45.20	Conor Dwyer — United States	1:45.23
2020 Tokyo	Tom Dean — Great Britain	1:44.22	Duncan Scott — Great Britain	1:44.26	Fernando Scheffer — Brazil	1:44.66
2024 Paris	David Popovici — Romania	1:44.72	Matthew Richards — Great Britain	1:44.74	Luke Hobson — United States	1:44.79

LIST OF OLYMPIC MEDALISTS IN SWIMMING

400 Metre Freestyle

Games	Gold		Silver		Bronze	
2000 Sydney	Ian Thorpe Australia	3:40.59 WR	Massimiliano Rosolino Italy	3:43.40	Klete Keller United States	3:47.00
2004 Athens	Ian Thorpe Australia	3:43.10	Grant Hackett Australia	3:43.36	Klete Keller United States	3:44.11
2008 Beijing	Park Tae-hwan South Korea	3:41.86	Zhang Lin China	3:42.44	Larsen Jensen United States	3:42.78
2012 London	Sun Yang China	3:40.14 OR	Park Tae-hwan South Korea	3:42.06	Peter Vanderkaay United States	3:44.69
2016 Rio de Janeiro	Mack Horton Australia	3:41.55	Sun Yang China	3:41.68	Gabriele Detti Italy	3:43.49
2020 Tokyo	Ahmed Hafnaoui Tunisia	3:43.36	Jack McLoughlin Australia	3:43.52	Kieran Smith United States	3:43.94
2024 Paris	Lukas Märtens Germany	3:41.78	Elijah Winnington Australia	3:42.21	Kim Woo-min South Korea	3:42.50

800 Metre freestyle

Games	Gold		Silver		Bronze	
2020 Tokyo	Bobby Finke United States	7:41.87	Gregorio Paltrinieri Italy	7:42.11	Mykhailo Romanchuk Ukraine	7:42.33 set OR in heats
2024 Paris	Daniel Wiffen Ireland	7:38.19 OR	Bobby Finke United States	7:38.75	Gregorio Paltrinieri Italy	7:39.38

LIST OF OLYMPIC MEDALISTS IN SWIMMING

1500 Metre freestyle

Games	Gold		Silver		Bronze	
2000 Sydney	Grant Hackett, Australia	14:48.33	Kieren Perkins, Australia	14:53.59	Chris Thompson, United States	14:56.81
2004 Athens	Grant Hackett, Australia	14:43.40 OR	Larsen Jensen, United States	14:45.29	David Davies, Great Britain	14:45.95
2008 Beijing	Oussama Mellouli, Tunisia	14:40.84	Grant Hackett, Australia	14:41.53 set OR in heats	Ryan Cochrane, Canada	14:42.69
2012 London	Sun Yang, China	14:31.02 WR	Ryan Cochrane, Canada	14:39.63	Oussama Mellouli, Tunisia	14:40.31
2016 Rio de Janeiro	Gregorio Paltrinieri, Italy	14:34.57	Connor Jaeger, United States	14:39.48	Gabriele Detti, Italy	14:40.86
2020 Tokyo	Bobby Finke, United States	14:39.65	Mykhailo Romanchuk, Ukraine	14:40.66	Florian Wellbrock, Germany	14:40.91
2024 Paris	Bobby Finke, United States	14:30.67 WR	Gregorio Paltrinieri, Italy	14:34.55	Daniel Wiffen, Ireland	14:39.63

100 Metre Backstroke

Games	Gold		Silver		Bronze	
2000 Sydney	Lenny Krayzelburg United States	53.72 OR	Matt Welsh Australia	54.07	Stev Theloke Germany	54.82
2004 Athens	Aaron Peirsol United States	54.06	Markus Rogan Austria	54.35	Tomomi Morita Japan	54.36
2008 Beijing	Aaron Peirsol United States	52.54 WR	Matt Grevers United States	53.11	Arkady Vyatchanin Russia Hayden Stoeckel Australia	53.18
2012 London	Matt Grevers United States	52.16 OR	Nick Thoman United States	52.92	Ryosuke Irie Japan	52.97
2016 Rio de Janeiro	Ryan Murphy United States	51.97 OR	Xu Jiayu China	52.31	David Plummer United States	52.40
2020 Tokyo	Evgeny Rylov ROC	51.98	Kliment Kolesnikov ROC	52.00	Ryan Murphy United States	52.19
2024 Paris	Thomas Ceccon Italy	52.00	Xu Jiayu China	52.32	Ryan Murphy United States	52.39

LIST OF OLYMPIC MEDALISTS IN SWIMMING

200 Metre Backstroke

Games	Gold		Silver		Bronze	
2000 Sydney	Lenny Krayzelburg United States	1:56.76 OR	Aaron Peirsol United States	1:57.35	Matt Welsh Australia	1:57.59
2004 Athens	Aaron Peirsol United States	1:54.95 OR	Markus Rogan Austria	1:57.35	Răzvan Florea Romania	1:57.56
2008 Beijing	Ryan Lochte United States	1:53.94 WR	Aaron Peirsol United States	1:54.33	Arkady Vyatchanin Russia	1:54.93
2012 London	Tyler Clary United States	1:53.41 OR	Ryosuke Irie Japan	1:53.78	Ryan Lochte United States	1:53.94
2016 Rio de Janeiro	Ryan Murphy United States	1:53.62	Mitch Larkin Australia	1:53.96	Evgeny Rylov Russia	1:53.97
2020 Tokyo	Evgeny Rylov ROC	1:53.27 OR	Ryan Murphy United States	1:54.15	Luke Greenbank Great Britain	1:54.72
2024 Paris	Hubert Kós Hungary	1:54.26	Apostolos Christou Greece	1:54.82	Roman Mityukov Switzerland	1:54.85

LIST OF OLYMPIC MEDALISTS (2000-2024)

100 Metre Breaststroke

Games	Gold		Silver		Bronze	
2000 Sydney	Domenico Fioravanti — Italy	1:00.46 OR	Ed Moses — United States	1:00.73	Roman Sloudnov — Russia	1:00.91
2004 Athens	Kosuke Kitajima — Japan	1:00.08	Brendan Hansen — United States	1:00.25 set OR in semifinal	Hugues Duboscq — France	1:00.88
2008 Beijing	Kosuke Kitajima — Japan	58.91 WR	Alexander Dale Oen — Norway	59.20	Hugues Duboscq — France	59.37
2012 London	Cameron van der Burgh — South Africa	58.46 WR	Christian Sprenger — Australia	58.93	Brendan Hansen — United States	59.49
2016 Rio de Janeiro	Adam Peaty — Great Britain	57.13 WR	Cameron van der Burgh — South Africa	58.69	Cody Miller — United States	58.87
2020 Tokyo	Adam Peaty — Great Britain	57.37	Arno Kamminga — Netherlands	58.00	Nicolò Martinenghi — Italy	58.33
2024 Paris	Nicolò Martinenghi — Italy	59.03	Adam Peaty — Great Britain / Nic Fink — United States	59.05		

200 Metre Breaststroke

Games	Gold		Silver		Bronze	
2000 Sydney	Domenico Fioravanti — Italy	2:10.87	Terence Parkin — South Africa	2:12.50	Davide Rummolo — Italy	2:12.73
2004 Athens	Kosuke Kitajima — Japan	2:09.44 OR	Dániel Gyurta — Hungary	2:10.80	Brendan Hansen — United States	2:10.87
2008 Beijing	Kosuke Kitajima — Japan	2:07.64 OR	Brenton Rickard — Australia	2:08.88	Hugues Duboscq — France	2:08.94
2012 London	Dániel Gyurta — Hungary	2:07.28 WR	Michael Jamieson — Great Britain	2:07.43	Ryo Tateishi — Japan	2:08.29
2016 Rio de Janeiro	Dmitriy Balandin — Kazakhstan	2:07.46	Josh Prenot — United States	2:07.53	Anton Chupkov — Russia	2:07.70
2020 Tokyo	Zac Stubblety-Cook — Australia	2:06.38 OR	Arno Kamminga — Netherlands	2:07.01	Matti Mattsson — Finland	2:07.13
2024 Paris	Léon Marchand — France	2:05.85 OR	Zac Stubblety-Cook — Australia	2:06.79	Caspar Corbeau — Netherlands	2:07.90

100 Metre Butterfly

Games	Gold		Silver		Bronze	
2000 Sydney	Lars Frölander Sweden	52.00	Michael Klim Australia	52.18	Geoff Huegill Australia	52.22
2004 Athens	Michael Phelps United States	51.25 **OR**	Ian Crocker United States	51.29	Andriy Serdinov Ukraine	51.36
2008 Beijing	Michael Phelps United States	50.58 **OR**	Milorad Čavić Serbia	50.59	Andrew Lauterstein Australia	51.12
2012 London	Michael Phelps United States	51.21	Chad le Clos South Africa Yevgeny Korotyshkin Russia	51.44	*none awarded*	
2016 Rio de Janeiro	Joseph Schooling Singapore	50.39 **OR**	László Cseh Hungary Chad le Clos South Africa Michael Phelps United States	51.14	*none awarded*	
2020 Tokyo	Caeleb Dressel United States	49.45 **WR**	Kristóf Milák Hungary	49.68	Noe Ponti Switzerland	50.74
2024 Paris	Kristóf Milák Hungary	49.90	Joshua Liendo Canada	49.99	Ilya Kharun Canada	50.45

200 Metre Butterfly

Games	Gold		Silver		Bronze	
2000 Sydney	Tom Malchow, United States	1:55.35 OR	Denys Sylantyev, Ukraine	1:55.76	Justin Norris, Australia	1:56.17
2004 Athens	Michael Phelps, United States	1:54.04 OR	Takashi Yamamoto, Japan	1:54.56	Steve Parry, Great Britain	1:55.52
2008 Beijing	Michael Phelps, United States	1:52.03 WR	László Cseh, Hungary	1:52.70	Takeshi Matsuda, Japan	1:52.97
2012 London	Chad le Clos, South Africa	1:52.96	Michael Phelps, United States	1:53.01	Takeshi Matsuda, Japan	1:53.21
2016 Rio de Janeiro	Michael Phelps, United States	1:53.36	Masato Sakai, Japan	1:53.40	Tamás Kenderesi, Hungary	1:53.62
2020 Tokyo	Kristóf Milák, Hungary	1:51.25 OR	Tomoru Honda, Japan	1:53.73	Federico Burdisso, Italy	1:54.45
2024 Paris	Léon Marchand, France	1:51.21 OR	Kristóf Milák, Hungary	1:51.75	Ilya Kharun, Canada	1:52.80

200 Metre Individual Medley

Games	Gold	Silver	Bronze
2000 Sydney	Massimiliano Rosolino Italy	Tom Dolan United States	Tom Wilkens United States
2004 Athens	Michael Phelps United States	Ryan Lochte United States	George Bovell Trinidad and Tobago
2008 Beijing	Michael Phelps United States	László Cseh Hungary	Ryan Lochte United States
2012 London	Michael Phelps United States	Ryan Lochte United States	László Cseh Hungary
2016 Rio de Janeiro	Michael Phelps United States	Kosuke Hagino Japan	Wang Shun China
2020 Tokyo	Wang Shun China	Duncan Scott Great Britain	Jérémy Desplanches Switzerland
2024 Paris	Léon Marchand France	Duncan Scott Great Britain	Wang Shun China

400 Metre Individual Medley

Games	Gold	Silver	Bronze
2000 Sydney	Tom Dolan United States	Erik Vendt United States	Curtis Myden Canada
2004 Athens	Michael Phelps United States	Erik Vendt United States	László Cseh Hungary
2008 Beijing	Michael Phelps United States	László Cseh Hungary	Ryan Lochte United States

LIST OF OLYMPIC MEDALISTS IN SWIMMING

Games	Gold	Silver	Bronze
2012 London	Ryan Lochte United States	Thiago Pereira Brazil	Kosuke Hagino Japan
2016 Rio de Janeiro	Kosuke Hagino Japan	Chase Kalisz United States	Daiya Seto Japan
2020 Tokyo	Chase Kalisz United States	Jay Litherland United States	Brendon Smith Australia
2024 Paris	Léon Marchand France	Tomoyuki Matsushita Japan	Carson Foster United States

4 × 100 Metre Freestyle Relay

Games	Gold	Silver	Bronze
2000 Sydney	Australia (AUS) Michael Klim Chris Fydler Ashley Callus Ian Thorpe Todd Pearson Adam Pine	United States (USA) Anthony Ervin Neil Walker Jason Lezak Gary Hall Jr. Scott Tucker Josh Davis	Brazil (BRA) Fernando Scherer Gustavo Borges Carlos Jayme Edvaldo Valério
2004 Athens	South Africa (RSA) Roland Schoeman Lyndon Ferns Darian Townsend Ryk Neethling	Netherlands (NED) Johan Kenkhuis Mitja Zastrow Klaas-Erik Zwering Pieter van den Hoogenband Mark Veens	United States (USA) Ian Crocker Michael Phelps Neil Walker Jason Lezak Gabe Woodward Nate Dusing Gary Hall Jr.

LIST OF OLYMPIC MEDALISTS (2000-2024)

Games	Gold	Silver	Bronze
2008 Beijing	United States (USA) Michael Phelps Garrett Weber-Gale Cullen Jones Jason Lezak Nathan Adrian Ben Wildman-Tobriner Matt Grevers	France (FRA) Amaury Leveaux Fabien Gilot Frédérick Bousquet Alain Bernard Grégory Mallet Boris Steimetz	Australia (AUS) Eamon Sullivan Andrew Lauterstein Ashley Callus Matt Targett Leith Brodie Patrick Murphy
2012 London *details*	France (FRA) Amaury Leveaux Fabien Gilot Clément Lefert Yannick Agnel Alain Bernard Jérémy Stravius	United States (USA) Nathan Adrian Michael Phelps Cullen Jones Ryan Lochte Jimmy Feigen Matt Grevers Ricky Berens Jason Lezak	Russia (RUS) Andrey Grechin Nikita Lobintsev Vladimir Morozov Danila Izotov Yevgeny Lagunov Sergey Fesikov
2016 Rio de Janeiro *details*	United States (USA) Caeleb Dressel Michael Phelps Ryan Held Nathan Adrian Jimmy Feigen Blake Pieroni Anthony Ervin	France (FRA) Mehdy Metella Fabien Gilot Florent Manaudou Jérémy Stravius Clément Mignon William Meynard	Australia (AUS) James Roberts Kyle Chalmers James Magnussen Cameron McEvoy Matthew Abood

LIST OF OLYMPIC MEDALISTS IN SWIMMING

Games	Gold	Silver	Bronze
2020 Tokyo *details*	🇺🇸 United States (USA) Caeleb Dressel Blake Pieroni Bowe Becker Zach Apple Brooks Curry	🇮🇹 Italy (ITA) Alessandro Miressi Thomas Ceccon Lorenzo Zazzeri Manuel Frigo Santo Condorelli	🇦🇺 Australia (AUS) Matthew Temple Zac Incerti Alexander Graham Kyle Chalmers Cameron McEvoy
2024 Paris *details*	🇺🇸 United States (USA) Jack Alexy Chris Guiliano Hunter Armstrong Caeleb Dressel Ryan Held Matthew King	🇦🇺 Australia (AUS) Jack Cartwright Flynn Southam Kai Taylor Kyle Chalmers William Yang	🇮🇹 Italy (ITA) Alessandro Miressi Thomas Ceccon Paolo Conte Bonin Manuel Frigo Lorenzo Zazzeri Leonardo Deplano

4 × 200 Metre Freestyle Relay

Games	Gold	Silver	Bronze
2000 Sydney	🇦🇺 Australia (AUS) Ian Thorpe Michael Klim Todd Pearson Bill Kirby Grant Hackett Daniel Kowalski	🇺🇸 United States (USA) Scott Goldblatt Josh Davis Jamie Rauch Klete Keller Nate Dusing Chad Carvin	🇳🇱 Netherlands (NED) Martijn Zuijdweg Johan Kenkhuis Marcel Wouda Pieter van den Hoogenband Mark van der Zijden

LIST OF OLYMPIC MEDALISTS (2000-2024)

Games	Gold	Silver	Bronze
2004 Athens	United States (USA) Michael Phelps Ryan Lochte Peter Vanderkaay Klete Keller Dan Ketchum Scott Goldblatt	Australia (AUS) Grant Hackett Michael Klim Nicholas Sprenger Ian Thorpe Todd Pearson Antony Matkovich Craig Stevens	Italy (ITA) Emiliano Brembilla Massimiliano Rosolino Simone Cercato Filippo Magnini Matteo Pelliciari Federico Cappellazzo
2008 Beijing	United States (USA) Michael Phelps Ryan Lochte Ricky Berens Peter Vanderkaay David Walters Erik Vendt Klete Keller	Russia (RUS) Danila Izotov Yevgeny Lagunov Nikita Lobintsev Alexander Sukhorukov Mikhail Polischuk	Australia (AUS) Patrick Murphy Grant Hackett Grant Brits Nick Ffrost Kirk Palmer Leith Brodie
2012 London	United States (USA) Ryan Lochte Conor Dwyer Ricky Berens Michael Phelps Charlie Houchin Matt McLean Davis Tarwater	France (FRA) Amaury Leveaux Grégory Mallet Clément Lefert Yannick Agnel Jérémy Stravius	China (CHN) Hao Yun Li Yunqi Jiang Haiqi Sun Yang Lü Zhiwu Dai Jun

LIST OF OLYMPIC MEDALISTS IN SWIMMING

Games	Gold	Silver	Bronze
2016 Rio de Janeiro	🇺🇸 United States (USA) Conor Dwyer Townley Haas Ryan Lochte Michael Phelps Clark Smith Jack Conger Gunnar Bentz	🇬🇧 Great Britain (GBR) Stephen Milne Duncan Scott Daniel Wallace James Guy Robbie Renwick	🇯🇵 Japan (JPN) Kosuke Hagino Naito Ehara Yuki Kobori Takeshi Matsuda
2020 Tokyo	🇬🇧 Great Britain (GBR) Tom Dean James Guy Matthew Richards Duncan Scott Calum Jarvis	ROC (ROC) Martin Malyutin Ivan Girev Evgeny Rylov Mikhail Dovgalyuk Aleksandr Krasnykh Mikhail Vekovishchev	🇦🇺 Australia (AUS) Alexander Graham Kyle Chalmers Zac Incerti Thomas Neill Mack Horton Elijah Winnington
2024 Paris	🇬🇧 Great Britain (GBR) James Guy Tom Dean Matthew Richards Duncan Scott Jack McMillan Kieran Bird	🇺🇸 United States (USA) Luke Hobson Carson Foster Drew Kibler Kieran Smith Brooks Curry Blake Pieroni Chris Guiliano	🇦🇺 Australia (AUS) Maximillian Giuliani Flynn Southam Elijah Winnington Thomas Neill Kai Taylor Zac Incerti

4 × 100 Metre Medley Relay

Games	Gold	Silver	Bronze
2000 Sydney	🇺🇸 United States (USA) Lenny Krayzelburg Ed Moses Ian Crocker Gary Hall Jr. Neil Walker Tommy Hannan Jason Lezak	🇦🇺 Australia (AUS) Matt Welsh Regan Harrison Geoff Huegill Michael Klim Josh Watson Ryan Mitchell Adam Pine Ian Thorpe	🇩🇪 Germany (GER) Stev Theloke Jens Kruppa Thomas Rupprath Torsten Spanneberg
2004 Athens	🇺🇸 United States (USA) Aaron Peirsol Brendan Hansen Ian Crocker Jason Lezak Lenny Krayzelburg Mark Gangloff Michael Phelps Neil Walker	🇩🇪 Germany (GER) Steffen Driesen Jens Kruppa Thomas Rupprath Lars Conrad Helge Meeuw	🇯🇵 Japan (JPN) Tomomi Morita Kosuke Kitajima Takashi Yamamoto Yoshihiro Okumura
2008 Beijing	🇺🇸 United States (USA) Aaron Peirsol Brendan Hansen Michael Phelps Jason Lezak Matt Grevers Mark Gangloff Ian Crocker Garrett Weber-Gale	🇦🇺 Australia (AUS) Hayden Stoeckel Brenton Rickard Andrew Lauterstein Eamon Sullivan Ashley Delaney Christian Sprenger Adam Pine Matt Targett	🇯🇵 Japan (JPN) Junichi Miyashita Kosuke Kitajima Takuro Fujii Hisayoshi Sato

LIST OF OLYMPIC MEDALISTS IN SWIMMING

Games	Gold	Silver	Bronze
2012 London	🇺🇸 United States (USA) Matt Grevers Brendan Hansen Michael Phelps Nathan Adrian Nick Thoman Eric Shanteau Tyler McGill Cullen Jones	🇯🇵 Japan (JPN) Ryosuke Irie Kosuke Kitajima Takeshi Matsuda Takuro Fujii	🇦🇺 Australia (AUS) Hayden Stoeckel Christian Sprenger Matt Targett James Magnussen Brenton Rickard Tommaso D'Orsogna
2016 Rio de Janeiro	🇺🇸 United States (USA) Ryan Murphy Cody Miller Michael Phelps Nathan Adrian David Plummer Kevin Cordes Tom Shields Caeleb Dressel	🇬🇧 Great Britain (GBR) Chris Walker-Hebborn Adam Peaty James Guy Duncan Scott	🇦🇺 Australia (AUS) Mitch Larkin Jake Packard David Morgan Kyle Chalmers Cameron McEvoy
2020 Tokyo	🇺🇸 United States (USA) Ryan Murphy Michael Andrew Caeleb Dressel Zach Apple Hunter Armstrong Blake Pieroni Tom Shields Andrew Wilson	🇬🇧 Great Britain (GBR) Luke Greenbank Adam Peaty James Guy Duncan Scott James Wilby	🇮🇹 Italy (ITA) Thomas Ceccon Nicolò Martinenghi Federico Burdisso Alessandro Miressi

Games	Gold	Silver	Bronze
2024 Paris	China (CHN) Xu Jiayu Qin Haiyang Sun Jiajun Pan Zhanle Wang Changhao	United States (USA) Ryan Murphy Nic Fink Caeleb Dressel Hunter Armstrong Charlie Swanson Thomas Heilman Jack Alexy	France (FRA) Yohann Ndoye-Brouard Léon Marchand Maxime Grousset Florent Manaudou Clément Secchi Rafael Fente-Damers

10 km Marathon

Games	Gold	Silver	Bronze
2008 Beijing	Maarten van der Weijden Netherlands	David Davies Great Britain	Thomas Lurz Germany
2012 London	Oussama Mellouli Tunisia	Thomas Lurz Germany	Richard Weinberger Canada
2016 Rio de Janeiro	Ferry Weertman Netherlands	Spyridon Gianniotis Greece	Marc-Antoine Olivier France
2020 Tokyo	Florian Wellbrock Germany	Kristof Rasovszky Hungary	Gregorio Paltrinieri Italy
2024 Paris	Kristóf Rasovszky Hungary	Oliver Klemet Germany	Dávid Betlehem Hungary

LIST OF OLYMPIC MEDALISTS IN SWIMMING

WOMEN

50 Metre Freestyle

Games	Gold	Silver	Bronze
2000 Sydney	Inge de Bruijn Netherlands	Therese Alshammar Sweden	Dara Torres United States
2004 Athens	Inge de Bruijn Netherlands	Malia Metella France	Libby Lenton Australia
2008 Beijing	Britta Steffen Germany	Dara Torres United States	Cate Campbell Australia
2012 London	Ranomi Kromowidjojo Netherlands	Aliaksandra Herasimenia Belarus	Marleen Veldhuis Netherlands
2016 Rio de Janeiro	Pernille Blume Denmark	Simone Manuel United States	Aliaksandra Herasimenia Belarus
2020 Tokyo	Emma McKeon Australia	Sarah Sjöström Sweden	Pernille Blume Denmark
2024 Paris	Sarah Sjöström Sweden	Meg Harris Australia	Zhang Yufei China

100 Metre Freestyle

Games	Gold	Silver	Bronze
2000 Sydney	Inge de Bruijn Netherlands	Therese Alshammar Sweden	Jenny Thompson United States / Dara Torres United States
2004 Athens	Jodie Henry Australia	Inge de Bruijn Netherlands	Natalie Coughlin United States

LIST OF OLYMPIC MEDALISTS (2000-2024)

Games	Gold	Silver	Bronze
2008 Beijing	Britta Steffen Germany	Lisbeth Trickett Australia	Natalie Coughlin United States
2012 London	Ranomi Kromowidjojo Netherlands	Aliaksandra Herasimenia Belarus	Tang Yi China
2016 Rio de Janeiro	Simone Manuel United States Penny Oleksiak Canada	none awarded	Sarah Sjöström Sweden
2020 Tokyo	Emma McKeon Australia	Siobhán Haughey Hong Kong	Cate Campbell Australia
2024 Paris	Sarah Sjöström Sweden	Torri Huske United States	Siobhán Haughey Hong Kong

200 Metre Freestyle

Games	Gold	Silver	Bronze
2000 Sydney	Susie O'Neill Australia	Martina Moravcová Slovakia	Claudia Poll Costa Rica
2004 Athens	Camelia Potec Romania	Federica Pellegrini Italy	Solenne Figuès France
2008 Beijing	Federica Pellegrini Italy	Sara Isaković Slovenia	Pang Jiaying China
2012 London	Allison Schmitt United States	Camille Muffat France	Bronte Barratt Australia

LIST OF OLYMPIC MEDALISTS IN SWIMMING

Games	Gold	Silver	Bronze
2016 Rio de Janeiro	Katie Ledecky United States	Sarah Sjöström Sweden	Emma McKeon Australia
2020 Tokyo	Ariarne Titmus Australia	Siobhán Haughey Hong Kong	Penny Oleksiak Canada
2024 Paris	Mollie O'Callaghan Australia	Ariarne Titmus Australia	Siobhán Haughey Hong Kong

400 Metre Freestyle

Games	Gold	Silver	Bronze
2000 Sydney	Brooke Bennett United States	Diana Munz United States	Claudia Poll Costa Rica
2004 Athens	Laure Manaudou France	Otylia Jędrzejczak Poland	Kaitlin Sandeno United States
2008 Beijing	Rebecca Adlington Great Britain	Katie Hoff United States	Joanne Jackson Great Britain
2012 London	Camille Muffat France	Allison Schmitt United States	Rebecca Adlington Great Britain
2016 Rio de Janeiro	Katie Ledecky United States	Jazmin Carlin Great Britain	Leah Smith United States
2020 Tokyo	Ariarne Titmus Australia	Katie Ledecky United States	Li Bingjie China

Games	Gold	Silver	Bronze
2024 Paris	Ariarne Titmus Australia	Summer McIntosh Canada	Katie Ledecky United States

800 Metre Freestyle

Games	Gold	Silver	Bronze
2000 Sydney	Brooke Bennett United States	Yana Klochkova Ukraine	Kaitlin Sandeno United States
2004 Athens	Ai Shibata Japan	Laure Manaudou France	Diana Munz United States
2008 Beijing	Rebecca Adlington Great Britain	Alessia Filippi Italy	Lotte Friis Denmark
2012 London	Katie Ledecky United States	Mireia Belmonte García Spain	Rebecca Adlington Great Britain
2016 Rio de Janeiro	Katie Ledecky United States	Jazmin Carlin Great Britain	Boglárka Kapás Hungary
2020 Tokyo	Katie Ledecky United States	Ariarne Titmus Australia	Simona Quadarella Italy
2024 Paris	Katie Ledecky United States	Ariarne Titmus Australia	Paige Madden United States

1500 Metre Freestyle

Games	Gold	Silver	Bronze
2020 Tokyo	Katie Ledecky 🇺🇸 United States	Erica Sullivan 🇺🇸 United States	Sarah Köhler 🇩🇪 Germany
2024 Paris	Katie Ledecky 🇺🇸 United States	Anastasiya Kirpichnikova 🇫🇷 France	Isabel Gose 🇩🇪 Germany

100 Metre Backstroke

Games	Gold	Silver	Bronze
2000 Sydney	Diana Mocanu 🇷🇴 Romania	Mai Nakamura 🇯🇵 Japan	Nina Zhivanevskaya 🇪🇸 Spain
2004 Athens	Natalie Coughlin 🇺🇸 United States	Kirsty Coventry 🇿🇼 Zimbabwe	Laure Manaudou 🇫🇷 France
2008 Beijing	Natalie Coughlin 🇺🇸 United States	Kirsty Coventry 🇿🇼 Zimbabwe	Margaret Hoelzer 🇺🇸 United States
2012 London	Missy Franklin 🇺🇸 United States	Emily Seebohm 🇦🇺 Australia	Aya Terakawa 🇯🇵 Japan
2016 Rio de Janeiro	Katinka Hosszú 🇭🇺 Hungary	Kathleen Baker 🇺🇸 United States	Fu Yuanhui 🇨🇳 China / Kylie Masse 🇨🇦 Canada
2020 Tokyo	Kaylee McKeown 🇦🇺 Australia	Kylie Masse 🇨🇦 Canada	Regan Smith 🇺🇸 United States
2024 Paris	Kaylee McKeown 🇦🇺 Australia	Regan Smith 🇺🇸 United States	Katharine Berkoff 🇺🇸 United States

200 Metre Backstroke

Games	Gold	Silver	Bronze
2000 Sydney	Diana Mocanu Romania	Roxana Maracineanu France	Miki Nakao Japan
2004 Athens	Kirsty Coventry Zimbabwe	Stanislava Komarova Russia	Antje Buschschulte Germany Reiko Nakamura Japan
2008 Beijing	Kirsty Coventry Zimbabwe	Margaret Hoelzer United States	Reiko Nakamura Japan
2012 London	Missy Franklin United States	Anastasia Zuyeva Russia	Elizabeth Beisel United States
2016 Rio de Janeiro	Maya DiRado United States	Katinka Hosszú Hungary	Hilary Caldwell Canada
2020 Tokyo	Kaylee McKeown Australia	Kylie Masse Canada	Emily Seebohm Australia
2024 Paris	Kaylee McKeown Australia	Regan Smith United States	Kylie Masse Canada

100 Metre Breaststroke

Games	Gold	Silver	Bronze
2000 Sydney	Megan Quann United States	Leisel Jones Australia	Penelope Heyns South Africa
2004 Athens	Luo Xuejuan China	Brooke Hanson Australia	Leisel Jones Australia
2008 Beijing	Leisel Jones Australia	Rebecca Soni United States	Mirna Jukić Austria

LIST OF OLYMPIC MEDALISTS IN SWIMMING

Games	Gold	Silver	Bronze
2012 London	Rūta Meilutytė Lithuania	Rebecca Soni United States	Satomi Suzuki Japan
2016 Rio de Janeiro	Lilly King United States	Yuliya Yefimova Russia	Katie Meili United States
2020 Tokyo	Lydia Jacoby United States	Tatjana Schoenmaker South Africa	Lilly King United States
2024 Paris	Tatjana Smith South Africa	Tang Qianting China	Mona McSharry Ireland

200 Metre Breaststroke

Games	Gold	Silver	Bronze
2000 Sydney	Ágnes Kovács Hungary	Kristy Kowal United States	Amanda Beard United States
2004 Athens	Amanda Beard United States	Leisel Jones Australia	Anne Poleska Germany
2008 Beijing	Rebecca Soni United States	Leisel Jones Australia	Sara Nordenstam Norway
2012 London	Rebecca Soni United States	Satomi Suzuki Japan	Yuliya Yefimova Russia
2016 Rio de Janeiro	Rie Kaneto Japan	Yuliya Yefimova Russia	Shi Jinglin China
2020 Tokyo	Tatjana Schoenmaker South Africa	Lilly King United States	Annie Lazor United States
2024 Paris	Kate Douglass United States	Tatjana Smith South Africa	Tes Schouten Netherlands

100 Metre Butterfly

Games	Gold	Silver	Bronze
2000 Sydney	Inge de Bruijn Netherlands	Martina Moravcová Slovakia	Dara Torres United States
2004 Athens	Petria Thomas Australia	Otylia Jędrzejczak Poland	Inge de Bruijn Netherlands
2008 Beijing	Lisbeth Trickett Australia	Christine Magnuson United States	Jessicah Schipper Australia
2012 London	Dana Vollmer United States	Lu Ying China	Alicia Coutts Australia
2016 Rio de Janeiro	Sarah Sjöström Sweden	Penny Oleksiak Canada	Dana Vollmer United States
2020 Tokyo	Maggie Mac Neil Canada	Zhang Yufei China	Emma McKeon Australia
2024 Paris	Torri Huske United States	Gretchen Walsh United States	Zhang Yufei China

200 Metre Butterfly

Games	Gold	Silver	Bronze
2000 Sydney	Misty Hyman United States	Susie O'Neill Australia	Petria Thomas Australia
2004 Athens	Otylia Jędrzejczak Poland	Petria Thomas Australia	Yuko Nakanishi Japan
2008 Beijing	Liu Zige China	Jiao Liuyang China	Jessicah Schipper Australia
2012 London	Jiao Liuyang China	Mireia Belmonte García Spain	Natsumi Hoshi Japan

| 2024 Paris | Summer McIntosh Canada | Kate Douglass United States | Kaylee McKeown Australia |

400 Metre Individual Medley

Games	Gold	Silver	Bronze
2000 Sydney	Yana Klochkova Ukraine	Yasuko Tajima Japan	Beatrice Câşlaru Romania
2004 Athens	Yana Klochkova Ukraine	Kaitlin Sandeno United States	Georgina Bardach Argentina
2008 Beijing	Stephanie Rice Australia	Kirsty Coventry Zimbabwe	Katie Hoff United States
2012 London	Ye Shiwen China	Elizabeth Beisel United States	Li Xuanxu China
2016 Rio de Janeiro	Katinka Hosszú Hungary	Maya DiRado United States	Mireia Belmonte García Spain
2020 Tokyo	Yui Ohashi Japan	Emma Weyant United States	Hali Flickinger United States
2024 Paris	Summer McIntosh Canada	Katie Grimes United States	Emma Weyant United States

Games	Gold	Silver	Bronze
2016 Rio de Janeiro	Mireia Belmonte García Spain	Madeline Groves Australia	Natsumi Hoshi Japan
2020 Tokyo	Zhang Yufei China	Regan Smith United States	Hali Flickinger United States
2024 Paris	Summer McIntosh Canada	Regan Smith United States	Zhang Yufei China

200 Metre Individual Medley

Games	Gold	Silver	Bronze
2000 Sydney	Yana Klochkova Ukraine	Beatrice Câşlaru Romania	Cristina Teuscher United States
2004 Athens	Yana Klochkova Ukraine	Amanda Beard United States	Kirsty Coventry Zimbabwe
2008 Beijing	Stephanie Rice Australia	Kirsty Coventry Zimbabwe	Natalie Coughlin United States
2012 London	Ye Shiwen China	Alicia Coutts Australia	Caitlin Leverenz United States
2016 Rio de Janeiro	Katinka Hosszú Hungary	Siobhan-Marie O'Connor Great Britain	Maya DiRado United States
2020 Tokyo	Yui Ohashi Japan	Alex Walsh United States	Kate Douglass United States

LIST OF OLYMPIC MEDALISTS IN SWIMMING

4 × 100 Metre Freestyle Relay

Games	Gold	Silver	Bronze
2000 Sydney	United States (USA) Amy Van Dyken Courtney Shealy Jenny Thompson Dara Torres Erin Phenix Ashley Tappin	Netherlands (NED) Manon van Rooijen Wilma van Hofwegen Inge de Bruijn Thamar Henneken Chantal Groot	Sweden (SWE) Johanna Sjöberg Therese Alshammar Louise Jöhncke Anna-Karin Kammerling Josefin Lillhage Malin Svahnström
2004 Athens	Australia (AUS) Alice Mills Libby Lenton Petria Thomas Jodie Henry Sarah Ryan	United States (USA) Kara Lynn Joyce Natalie Coughlin Amanda Weir Jenny Thompson Colleen Lanne Maritza Correia Lindsay Benko	Netherlands (NED) Chantal Groot Inge Dekker Marleen Veldhuis Inge de Bruijn Annabel Kosten
2008 Beijing	Netherlands (NED) Inge Dekker Ranomi Kromowidjojo Femke Heemskerk Marleen Veldhuis Hinkelien Schreuder Manon van Rooijen	United States (USA) Natalie Coughlin Dara Torres Kara Lynn Joyce Lacey Nymeyer Emily Silver Julia Smit	Australia (AUS) Cate Campbell Alice Mills Melanie Schlanger Lisbeth Trickett Shayne Reese

Games	Gold	Silver	Bronze
2012 London	Australia (AUS) Alicia Coutts Cate Campbell Brittany Elmslie Melanie Schlanger Emily Seebohm Yolane Kukla Lisbeth Trickett	Netherlands (NED) Inge Dekker Marleen Veldhuis Femke Heemskerk Ranomi Kromowidjojo Hinkelien Schreuder	United States (USA) Missy Franklin Jessica Hardy Lia Neal Allison Schmitt Amanda Weir Natalie Coughlin
2016 Rio de Janeiro	Australia (AUS) Emma McKeon Brittany Elmslie Bronte Campbell Cate Campbell Madison Wilson	United States (USA) Simone Manuel Abbey Weitzeil Dana Vollmer Katie Ledecky Amanda Weir Lia Neal Allison Schmitt	Canada (CAN) Sandrine Mainville Chantal Van Landeghem Taylor Ruck Penny Oleksiak Michelle Williams
2020 Tokyo	Australia (AUS) Bronte Campbell Meg Harris Emma McKeon Cate Campbell Mollie O'Callaghan Madison Wilson	Canada (CAN) Kayla Sanchez Margaret MacNeil Rebecca Smith Penny Oleksiak Taylor Ruck	United States (USA) Erika Brown Abbey Weitzeil Natalie Hinds Simone Manuel Olivia Smoliga Catie DeLoof Allison Schmitt

LIST OF OLYMPIC MEDALISTS IN SWIMMING

Games	Gold	Silver	Bronze
2024 Paris	Australia (AUS) Mollie O'Callaghan Shayna Jack Emma McKeon Meg Harris Olivia Wunsch Bronte Campbell	United States (USA) Kate Douglass Gretchen Walsh Torri Huske Simone Manuel Abbey Weitzeil Erika Connolly	China (CHN) Yang Junxuan Cheng Yujie Zhang Yufei Wu Qingfeng Yu Yiting

4 × 200 Metre Freestyle Relay

Games	Gold	Silver	Bronze
2000 Sydney	United States (USA) Diana Munz Jenny Thompson Samantha Arsenault Lindsay Benko Julia Stowers Kim Black	Australia (AUS) Giaan Rooney Petria Thomas Kirsten Thomson Susie O'Neill Jacinta van Lint Elka Graham	Germany (GER) Franziska van Almsick Antje Buschschulte Sara Harstick Kerstin Kielgass Meike Freitag Britta Steffen
2004 Athens	United States (USA) Natalie Coughlin Carly Piper Dana Vollmer Kaitlin Sandeno Lindsay Benko Rhi Jeffrey Rachel Komisarz	China (CHN) Zhu Yingwen Xu Yanwei Yang Yu Pang Jiaying Li Ji	Germany (GER) Franziska van Almsick Petra Dallmann Antje Buschschulte Hannah Stockbauer Janina Götz Sara Harstick

LIST OF OLYMPIC MEDALISTS (2000-2024)

Games	Gold	Silver	Bronze
2008 Beijing	Australia (AUS) Stephanie Rice Bronte Barratt Kylie Palmer Linda Mackenzie Felicity Galvez Angie Bainbridge Melanie Schlanger Lara Davenport	China (CHN) Yang Yu Zhu Qianwei Tan Miao Pang Jiaying Tang Jingzhi	United States (USA) Allison Schmitt Natalie Coughlin Caroline Burckle Katie Hoff Christine Marshall Kim Vandenberg Julia Smit
2012 London	United States (USA) Missy Franklin Dana Vollmer Shannon Vreeland Allison Schmitt Lauren Perdue Alyssa Anderson	Australia (AUS) Bronte Barratt Melanie Schlanger Kylie Palmer Alicia Coutts Brittany Elmslie Angie Bainbridge Jade Neilsen Blair Evans	France (FRA) Camille Muffat Charlotte Bonnet Ophélie-Cyrielle Étienne Coralie Balmy Margaux Farrell Mylène Lazare
2016 Rio de Janeiro	United States (USA) Allison Schmitt Leah Smith Maya DiRado Katie Ledecky Missy Franklin Melanie Margalis Cierra Runge	Australia (AUS) Leah Neale Emma McKeon Bronte Barratt Tamsin Cook Jessica Ashwood	Canada (CAN) Katerine Savard Taylor Ruck Brittany MacLean Penny Oleksiak Emily Overholt Kennedy Goss

LIST OF OLYMPIC MEDALISTS IN SWIMMING

Games	Gold	Silver	Bronze
2020 Tokyo	🇨🇳 China (CHN) Yang Junxuan Tang Muhan Zhang Yufei Li Bingjie Zhang Yifan Dong Jie	🇺🇸 United States (USA) Allison Schmitt Paige Madden Katie McLaughlin Katie Ledecky Bella Sims Brooke Forde	🇦🇺 Australia (AUS) Ariarne Titmus Emma McKeon Madison Wilson Leah Neale Mollie O'Callaghan Meg Harris Brianna Throssell Tamsin Cook
2024 Paris	🇦🇺 Australia Mollie O'Callaghan Lani Pallister Brianna Throssell Ariarne Titmus Jamie Perkins Shayna Jack	🇺🇸 United States Claire Weinstein Paige Madden Katie Ledecky Erin Gemmell Anna Peplowski Simone Manuel Alex Shackell	🇨🇳 China Yang Junxuan Li Bingjie Ge Chutong Liu Yaxin Tang Muhan Kong Yaqi

4 × 100 Metre Medley Relay

Games	Gold	Silver	Bronze
2000 Sydney	🇺🇸 United States (USA) Dara Torres Barbara Bedford Megan Quann Jenny Thompson Courtney Shealy Ashley Tappin Amy Van Dyken Staciana Stitts	🇦🇺 Australia (AUS) Petria Thomas Leisel Jones Susie O'Neill Dyana Calub Giaan Rooney Tarnee White Sarah Ryan	🔴 Japan (JPN) Masami Tanaka Sumika Minamoto Mai Nakamura Junko Onishi
2004 Athens	🇦🇺 Australia (AUS) Giaan Rooney Leisel Jones Petria Thomas Jodie Henry Brooke Hanson Jessicah Schipper Alice Mills	🇺🇸 United States (USA) Natalie Coughlin Amanda Beard Jenny Thompson Kara Lynn Joyce Haley Cope Tara Kirk Rachel Komisarz Amanda Weir	🇩🇪 Germany (GER) Antje Buschschulte Sarah Poewe Franziska van Almsick Daniela Götz
2008 Beijing	🇦🇺 Australia (AUS) Emily Seebohm Leisel Jones Jessicah Schipper Lisbeth Trickett Tarnee White Felicity Galvez Shayne Reese	🇺🇸 United States (USA) Natalie Coughlin Rebecca Soni Christine Magnuson Dara Torres Margaret Hoelzer Megan Jendrick Elaine Breeden Kara Lynn Joyce	🇨🇳 China (CHN) Zhao Jing Sun Ye Zhou Yafei Pang Jiaying Xu Tianlongzi

LIST OF OLYMPIC MEDALISTS IN SWIMMING

Games	Gold	Silver	Bronze
2012 London	United States (USA) Missy Franklin Rebecca Soni Dana Vollmer Allison Schmitt Rachel Bootsma Breeja Larson Claire Donahue Jessica Hardy	Australia (AUS) Emily Seebohm Leisel Jones Alicia Coutts Melanie Schlanger Brittany Elmslie	Japan (JPN) Aya Terakawa Satomi Suzuki Yuka Kato Haruka Ueda
2016 Rio de Janeiro	United States (USA) Kathleen Baker Lilly King Dana Vollmer Simone Manuel Olivia Smoliga Katie Meili Kelsi Worrell Abbey Weitzeil	Australia (AUS) Emily Seebohm Taylor McKeown Emma McKeon Cate Campbell Madison Wilson Madeline Groves Brittany Elmslie	Denmark (DEN) Mie Nielsen Rikke Møller Pedersen Jeanette Ottesen Pernille Blume
2020 Tokyo	Australia (AUS) Kaylee McKeown Chelsea Hodges Emma McKeon Cate Campbell Emily Seebohm Brianna Throssell Mollie O'Callaghan	United States (USA) Regan Smith Lydia Jacoby Torri Huske Abbey Weitzeil Rhyan White Lilly King Claire Curzan Erika Brown	Canada (CAN) Kylie Masse Sydney Pickrem Maggie Mac Neil Penny Oleksiak Taylor Ruck Kayla Sanchez

Games	Gold	Silver	Bronze
2024 Paris	United States (USA) Regan Smith Lilly King Gretchen Walsh Torri Huske Katharine Berkoff Emma Weber Alex Shackell Kate Douglass	Australia (AUS) Kaylee McKeown Jenna Strauch Emma McKeon Mollie O'Callaghan Iona Anderson Ella Ramsay Alexandria Perkins Meg Harris	China (CHN) Wan Letian Tang Qianting Zhang Yufei Yang Junxuan Wang Xue'er Yu Yiting Wu Qingfeng